WHISPERING WALLS

FIRST WORLD WAR GRAFFITI

DAVID CROSSLAND

AMBERLEY

First published 2023

Amberley Publishing
The Hill, Stroud,
Gloucestershire, GL5 4EP

www.amberley-books.com

ISBN: 978 1 3981 1188 2 (print)
ISBN: 978 1 3981 1189 9 (ebook)

British Library Cataloguing in Publication Data.
A catalogue record for this book is available from the British Library.

Typeset in 10pt on 13pt Celeste.
Typesetting by SJmagic DESIGN SERVICES, India.
Printed in the UK.

Contents

A Hidden Legacy

When you walk around a war cemetery in northern France, the mass of headstones stretching into the distance can obscure that each grave stands for a life lived and a dream dreamt. The generation that fell silent on the Western Front over a century ago is often remembered collectively rather than as individuals.

However, their voices are being heard again from beneath the battlefields in the form of graffiti rediscovered in limestone quarries where many thousands of soldiers from both

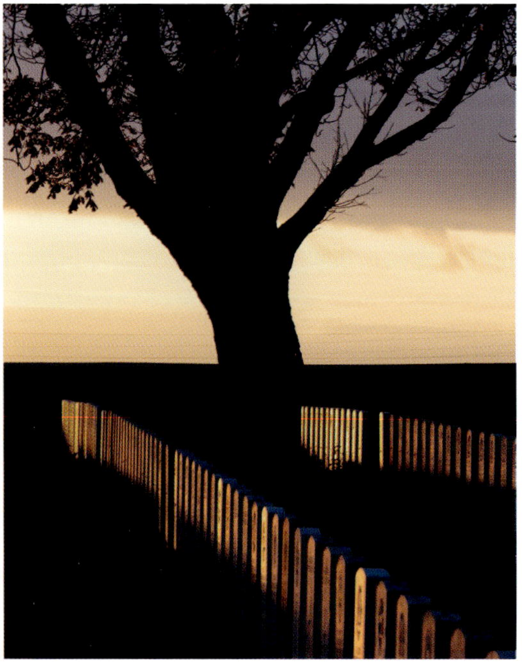

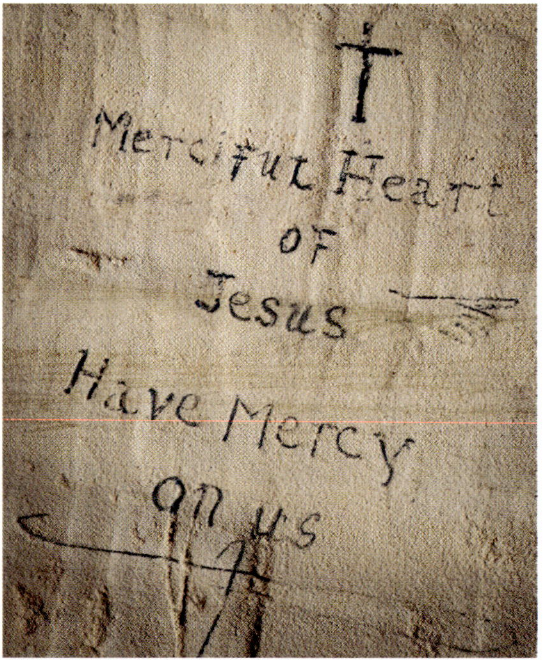

Above left: British war graves in Cabaret Rouge cemetery, near Arras.

Above right: Inscription by an American soldier.

sides sheltered. On the walls of long forgotten time-warp tunnels strewn with bully beef tins and boots, markings ranging from hastily scribbled names to elaborate carvings betray the soldiers' emotions as they waited to go into battle.

Down here in the gloom their thoughts were free to roam for a few minutes, hours or days. The outcome is a deeply personal and immediate testimony. The men knew that their inscription might be their last trace – in very many cases, it was. So they wrote their name, rank and service number, and sometimes even their home address. Or the name of a mate who had fallen. Or they created portraits of their wife or girlfriend, or that pretty mademoiselle they saw in that estaminet last month. Their farm animals back home, their favourite horse or dog. A rousing poem. A sarcastic remark. A patriotic slogan. A Christian cross.

Using their knives, bayonets, or pencils, they copied the insignia of their regiment or battalion into the soft stone. They carved four-leafed clovers for luck, the Square and Compasses of their Masonic lodge or symbols of their nation such as Nelson's Column, Marianne, the Iron Cross, the Canadian Maple Leaf or Native American profiles with feather headdresses.

The inscriptions reflect the variety of cultures that converged on the battlefields of France. But they illustrate just as clearly what all the combatants had in common: a will to survive, to return to their loved ones, to be remembered, to prove their worth.

Many of the carvings are so intricate that they must have taken hours of concentrated effort, revealing the mental resilience of young people clinging to happiness and hope amid the bloody turmoil. Of course, some of the artworks depict big-breasted nudes or male genitals. This was graffiti after all, created by boys in their teens and twenties.

The inscriptions represent a moment. They are completely undistorted by time. They cut through decades of myth, propaganda and shifting trends of remembrance. Over a century on, they speak directly to the viewer. Not, 'this is what it was like.' But 'this is what it *is* like.' They provide new insights not just into the war but the human response to extreme conflict.

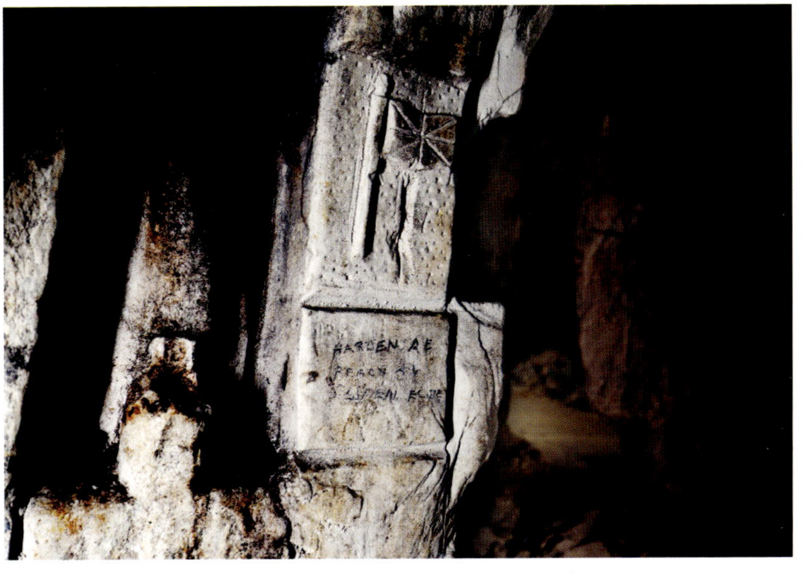

The Maison Blanche quarry near Arras.

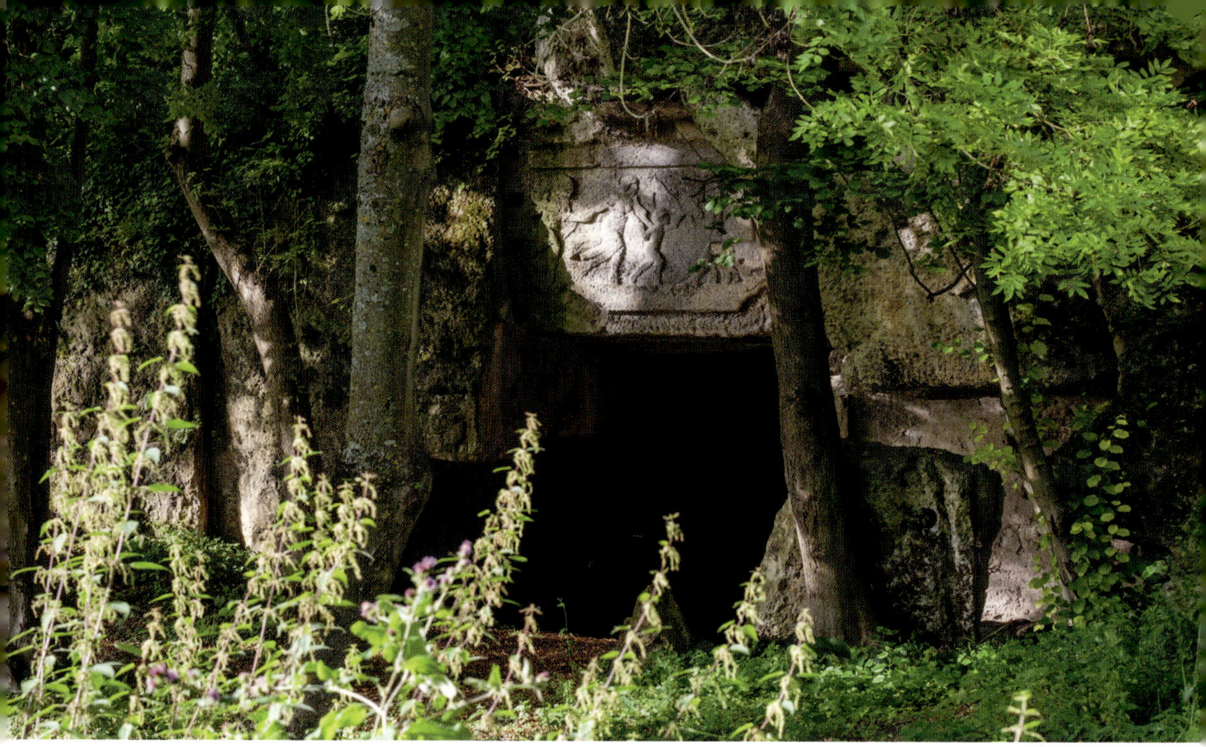

The entrance to a quarry at Confrécourt used by the French army.

Individual though they are, each one resounds with the question 'will I live?'

Standing where they stood as we admire their work, tasting the chalk dust floating in the torchlight, we can answer that question today. All too often, it is a shake of the head, and the young artists are found lying in a cemetery, sometimes just a few kilometres away. That makes venturing into these hidden tunnels poignant and humbling.

There are an estimated 400 quarries with significant quantities of graffiti in the Hauts-de-France region comprising the Arras, Somme, Aisne and Oise battle sectors. Almost every village and town has one, dug by farmers centuries ago as a source of limestone used to build houses and churches. They would dig a shaft known as a 'puit' into a field or a ridge and fan out underground from there, creating labyrinthine networks of tunnels and chambers as they extracted the slabs cut out of the rock.

These sites, mostly dug in the Middle Ages but some dating back to Roman times, became useful as hiding places for villagers during the wars that ravaged the region over the centuries. They went out of use as quarries in the nineteenth century, but the air of secrecy surrounding them persists to this day. Many are crumbling and dangerous to visit, their entrances blocked by rusting gates or well concealed in wooded slopes.

After the French and British pushed the Germans back from Paris in September 1914 and the Germans dug in on high ground across Picardy, the quarries were discovered by both sides as ideal locations for unit headquarters, field hospitals and troop accommodation. The British called them 'caves' and the Germans 'höhlen.' The French refer to them as souterraines, carrières or creutes.

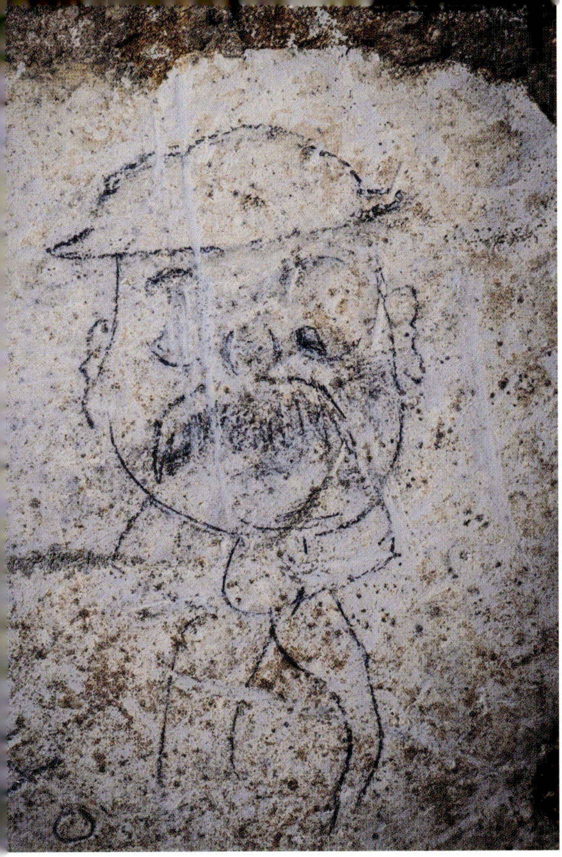

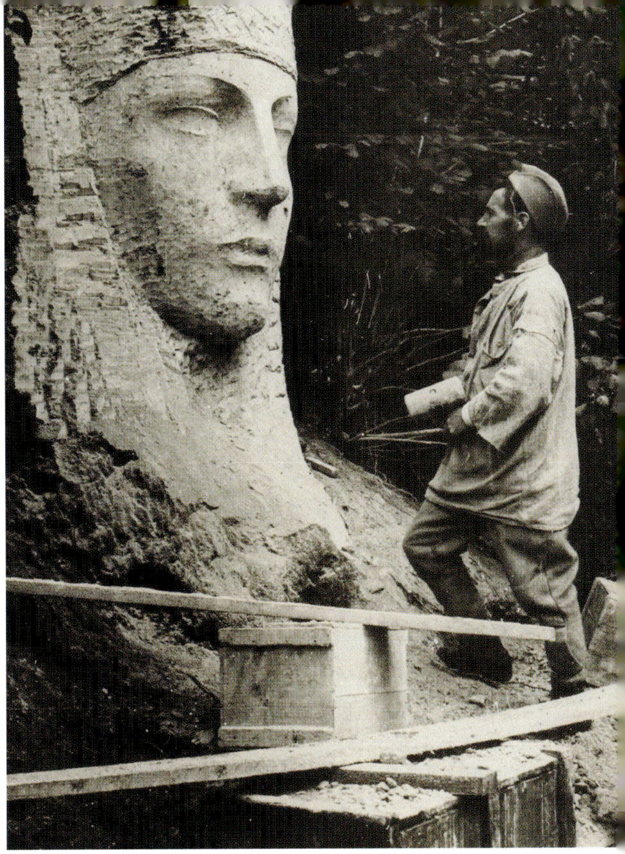

Above left: Drawing of the popular British First World War cartoon character 'Old Bill' depicting an elderly Tommy on the wall of a quarry in Habarcq, west of Arras. The signature next to it is by Private Alfred Honour of the Royal Army Medical Corps, service number 19666.

Above right: The French professional sculptor Louis Leclabart, who was a stretcher-bearer during the war, working on a sculpture of the Sphinx at a quarry near Thiescourt in September 1916. It still exists, minus its nose. (La Contemporaine VAL 269/173 Producer: Section photographique de l'armée)

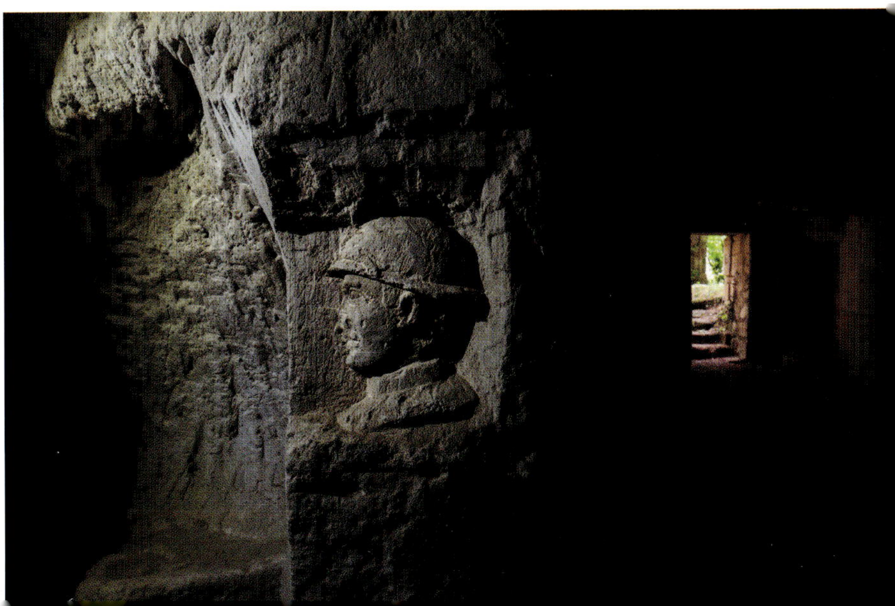

Bas-relief of a French soldier in the bowels of the ancient fortress-like Ferme de Confrécourt.

Research into the underground graffiti has intensified in recent years, fuelled by resurgent interest in the First World War over the centenary and the realisation that this is a fragile legacy whose years are numbered.

The digitisation of military records has made it easy to trace the fate of thousands of soldiers who made their mark. Enlistment forms and battalion war diaries enable us to piece together their passage through the trenches and into no man's land, establishing a direct link with the past. Families from as far away as Australia have been notified of their ancestors' inscriptions and have made pilgrimages to attach poppies to the walls.

Fascinating stories hidden underground for over a century have come to light, conveying the cost of war as powerfully as cemeteries and memorials. The Antarctic explorer who used his surveying skills to map battlefields. The opera baritone who chiselled patriotic sculptures. The Victoria Cross winner thrust into the glaring limelight. The aircraft mechanic who guarded the Red Baron's body. The inseparable brothers torn apart. The wounded mountaineer who reconquered the peaks of his homeland. The corporal saved from shrapnel by his breast pocket Bible.

Some caves changed hands repeatedly as the front line shifted, and it is striking that troops from both sides respected each other's graffiti. There are examples of a French name written on the same piece of rock as a German one.

Expressions of hatred for the enemy are conspicuously rare. After all, the artists, mostly ordinary soldiers rather than officers, knew that they were all going through the same hell.

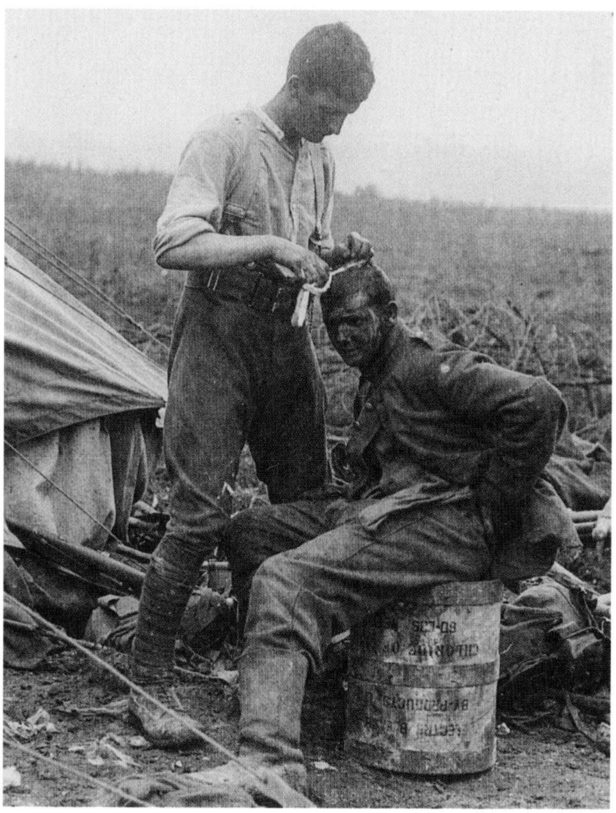

British soldier bandaging a German prisoner at Bernafay, Somme, 19 July 1916. (La Contemporaine VAL 439/005 Producer: British official photo)

I Was Here

For a few hours they were tourists, wandering through a labyrinth of man-made caves under the village of Naours, enjoying a respite from the trenches to the east. Ten thousand miles from home, they pencilled their names, ranks and units on the walls in the torch-lit gloom.

Among them was Lance-Corporal Adrian Henry Edmonds of the 3rd Australian Division Signals Company. He came to Naours on 23 May 1917 and was impressed by what he saw.

Lance-Corporal Adrian Henry Edmonds' inscription at Naours.

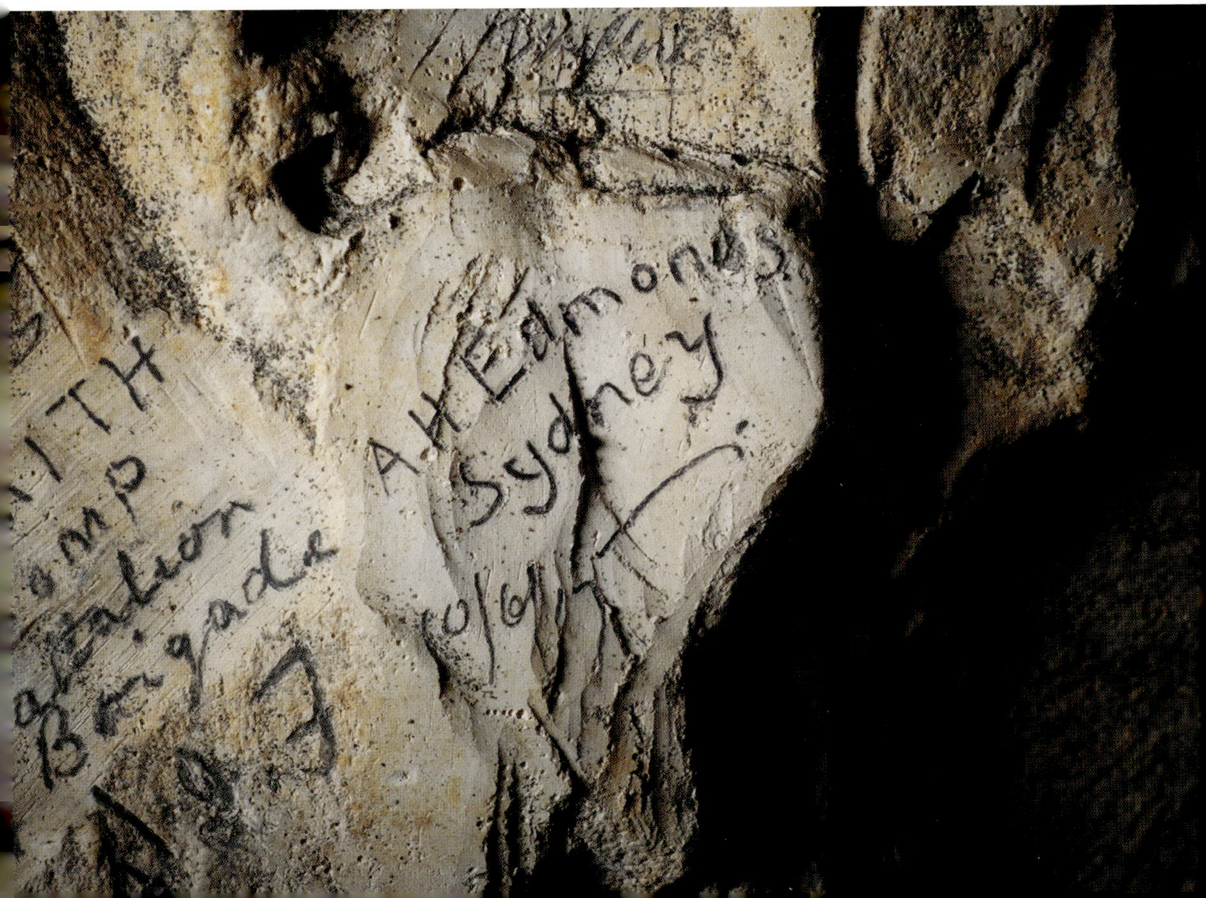

'These historic excavations made about 850 years ago for protection of inhabitants during an invasion,' he wrote in his diary. Edmonds, in his mid-twenties, from Sydney, a clerk in civilian life, had a dangerous job – laying telephone lines across battlefields – but he was also a keen sightseer.

He was among thousands of mainly Australian soldiers who visited Naours and signed the rock walls. The underground city less than 20 kilometres north of Amiens boasts the biggest concentration of soldiers' graffiti from the First World War yet found in France. Their significance has only been recognised since 2014 when the French archaeologist Gilles Prilaux came across the trove of inscriptions while examining the network of galleries and 130 chambers. 'I was inspecting the ground and found patches of burnt earth with coal dating back to the time of the Thirty Years War, coins, musket balls and ceramic shards,' said Prilaux. 'The story could have ended there but I looked up and saw some writing on the wall. A name, a service number and 59th Battalion. And I noticed there were hundreds of similar inscriptions on the walls. It's incredible but for decades until 2014, people had been brushing past these pencil markings in the gloom without noticing them. So I decided to research this site.'

At first, it was like deciphering hieroglyphs. Prilaux learned that NSW means New South Wales, VC stands for the state of Victoria and COY meant Company. The soldiers copied each other, preparing a flat surface on the soft limestone with a knife and then writing their inscription, sometimes with normal lead pencils and sometimes with purple ink pencils, with the latter being less well preserved a century on because the ink has become absorbed by the chalk. The names were found in concentrations in certain parts

Some 3,200 names have been logged on the walls of Naours, including those of 2,200 Australian soldiers.

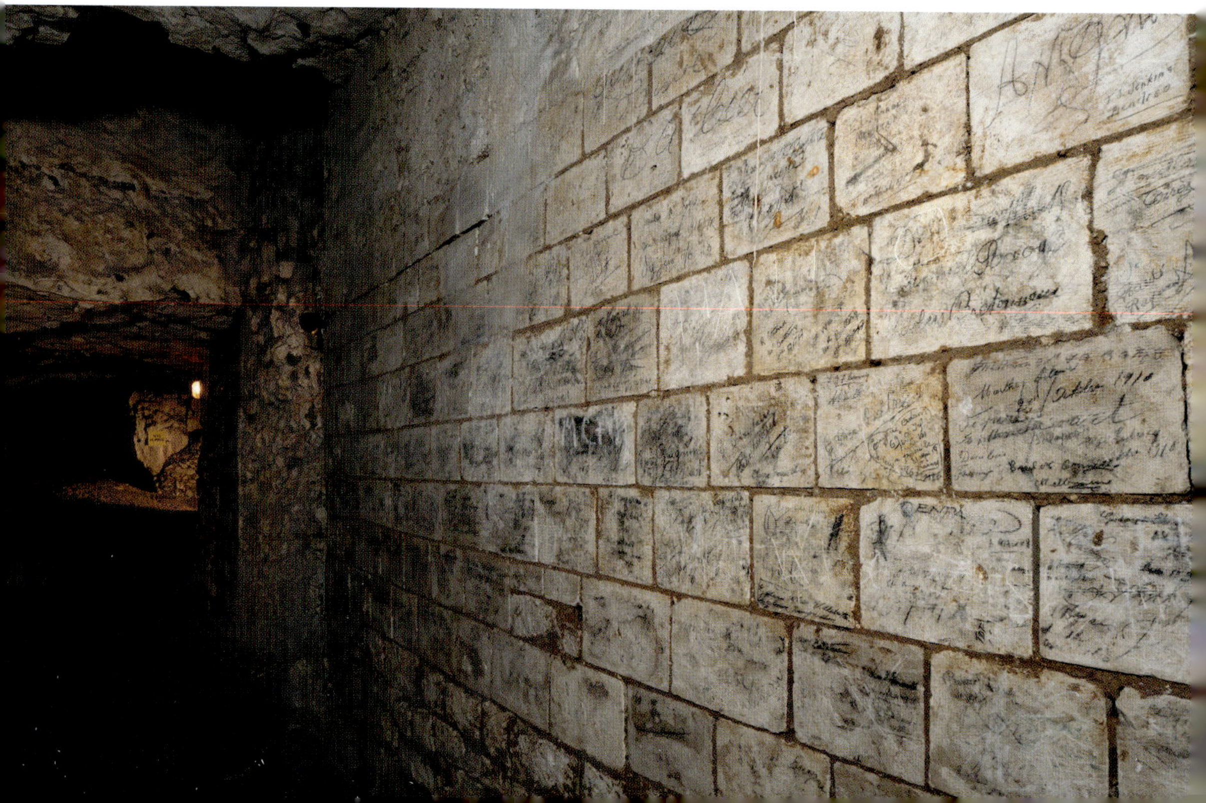

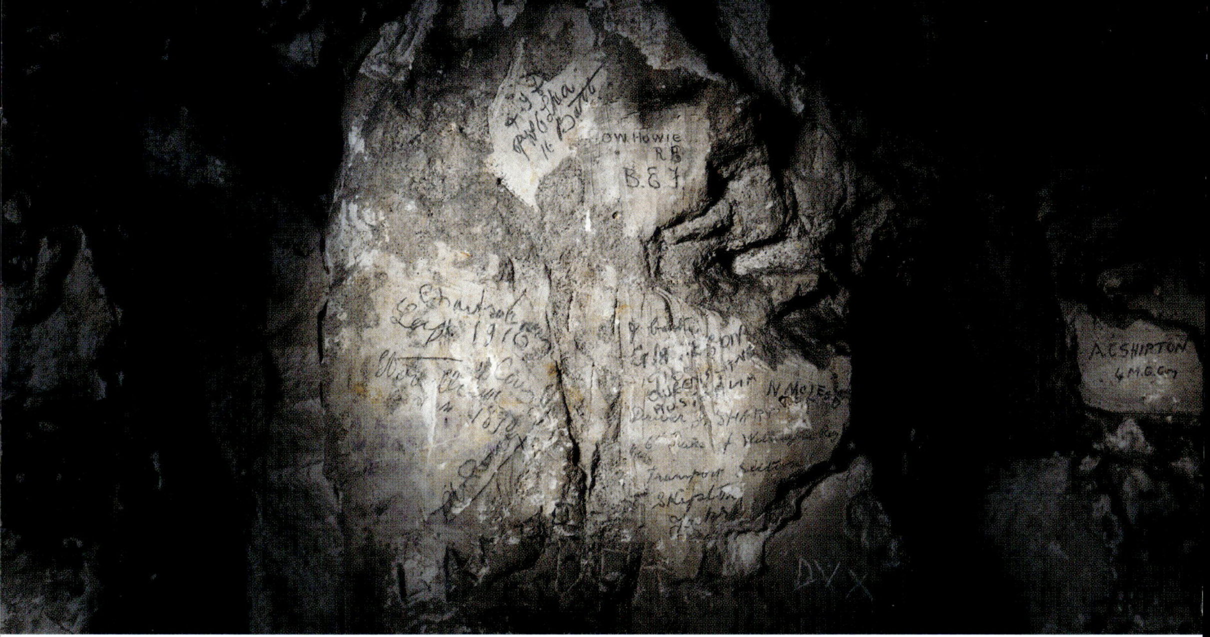

Above: There are especially many inscriptions in parts of the network where the Naours tour guides made stops.

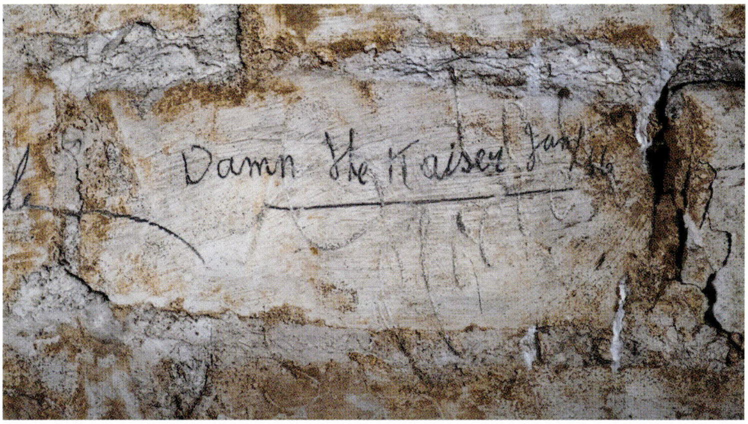

Right: Inscriptions like this one expressing hostility towards the enemy are rare.

of the complex, probably where the guide made a stop, which would give the soldiers the opportunity to write on the walls.

In his diary, Lance-Corporal Edmonds conveyed both the horror of the fighting and the beauty of the landscapes he travelled through. In July 1916, on a troop train taking his unit to the Somme, he wrote of 'hills covered with wheat interspersed with red poppies and cornflowers.' The River Somme, he noted on 12 July, was 'bordered with beautiful trees.' A few weeks later, on 29 July, he wrote: 'Very heavy shelling all day and many casualties, there are some awful sights – half bodies, legs, arms etc. lying about unburied.' He complained about the 'awful stench' and the 'myriads of black loathsome flies' in the

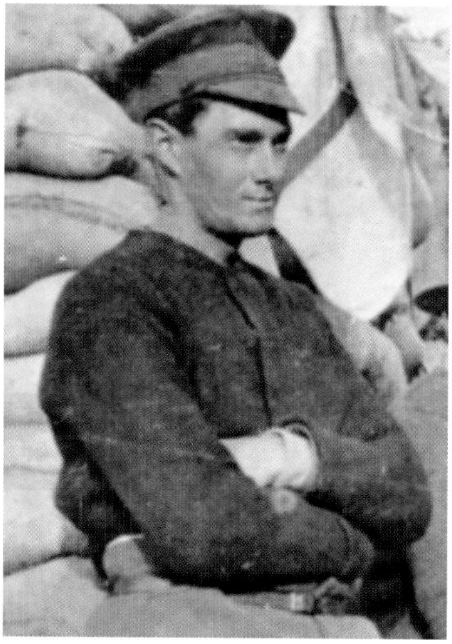

Adrian Henry Edmonds in Gallipoli in September 1915. (Australian War Memorial)

destroyed Somme village of Pozières, one of the crucibles of the Australian Imperial Force (AIF), where men's legs, arms and heads stuck out of the sides of his trench. A week later, he was billeted in the village of Beauval and noted its 'fine Gothic church.'

In November that year he wrote of pack animals lying dead by the roadside, shot by their handlers who could not extricate them from the mud. 'We are drinking water out of shell holes [that] has a flavour of dead bodies, in fact some of the holes have a mixture of blood and water,' he wrote. 9 November saw 'lively bombardment on and off all day.' He added: 'Outside our trenches in no man's land are scores of Australian dead killed in the last charge. It is pure murder to order a charge over this terrible ground, it is too slippery to stand on much less charge over.' On 17 November, he wrote of having shivered all night with only one blanket, but he spared a thought for the 'poor horses' struggling over the frozen mud. He was without rations the next day because the pack mule had failed to arrive. 'Shell hole water past drinking.' On Boxing Day 1916, he took a walk in Delville Wood, one of the bloodiest battlegrounds of the Somme in the summer.

'Shattered trees and trenches, shell holes, military gear and corpses by the score are scattered everywhere. British and Germans mixed some with bayonets through their bodies, others with limbs blown off – facts which show only too plainly the terrible contest for this Wood which the British captured on 27 July 1916. If only those who are responsible for this terrible war could see these silent forms!'

Edmonds' job was to set up field communications using cables, radio and visual signalling like flags and lamps. Comrades of his were wounded and killed. During the Third Battle of Ypres, he was almost burned alive when a shell landed on a dump of flares near the door to his bunker and set them alight, sending flames and fumes sweeping in through the only exit. He recalled a dog fight between Allied and German planes – 'the excitement was so tense that the artillery stopped firing to watch' – and the 'delightful odour of a dozen roast Fritzes' inside a German redoubt his unit took after it had been set on fire by a bomb.

Then, a few weeks later, on leave in Paris, he listed the sights he had ticked off: the Place de Vendome, the Invalides with Napoleon's tomb, the Eiffel Tower and a visit to the Folies Bergère. He even took in Versailles to round off what he described as 'a perfect holiday.'

Edmonds survived the war and returned home in 1919. He died in 1968.

The brothers Percy Augustine Ellis and Abel Ellis of the 14th Battalion of the Australian Infantry etched their names in big letters at Naours on 24 July 1916. Fifteen days later, in the early morning of 8 August in fighting at Pozières, both were buried by a shell that struck their trench. 'Brother dug-out alright but A. Ellis died a minute after being dug-out,' an eyewitness reported, according to an Australian military record. Eight months later, in April 1917, Percy was wounded by a bullet to the right shoulder at Bullecourt, taken prisoner by the Germans and treated in a hospital in Stettin, now the Polish city of Szczecin. He was repatriated to England in December 1918, married in 1921 and died in 1925 of tuberculosis. Two other Ellis brothers also served in the war and survived.

Naours is unique because it was a tourist attraction during the war and remains so to this day. The Australian army in particular laid on excursions. Among the sightseers was Leslie Russell Blake, a lieutenant in the 105th Howitzer Battery of the 5th Australian Field Artillery. He wrote his name on a wall there on 7 January 1917. Prilaux came across the inscription almost a century later and traced it back to the adventurous surveyor and geologist who had spent the last pre-war years on an Antarctic expedition under the explorer Douglas Mawson, a peer of Shackleton and Scott. Twenty-six at the time, handsome, blue-eyed and 5 feet 8½ inches tall, Blake arrived in France as a Second Lieutenant and was in charge of a 4.5 inch howitzer. But his surveying skills were what set him apart. In July 1916, months before he visited Naours, he had ventured into no man's land in front of Pozières, tasked with surveying the exact location of the Allied lines. The precarious mission during which he was wounded by a sniper was crucial to prepare the artillery for an accurate creeping barrage of fire behind which the troops were able to

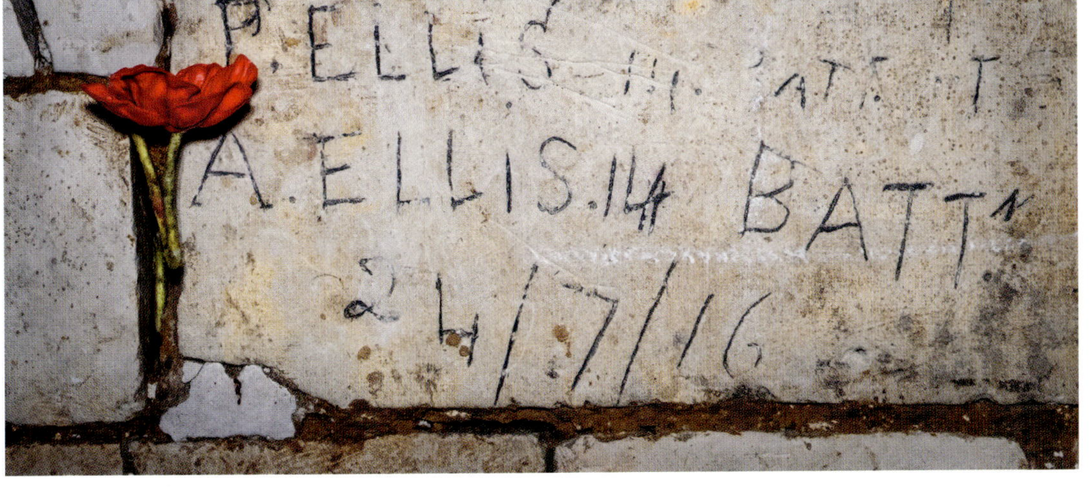

Families from Australia on the far side of the world have come to Naours to stand where their ancestors stood and see the inscriptions they left. Abel Ellis was killed fifteen days after this inscription was made.

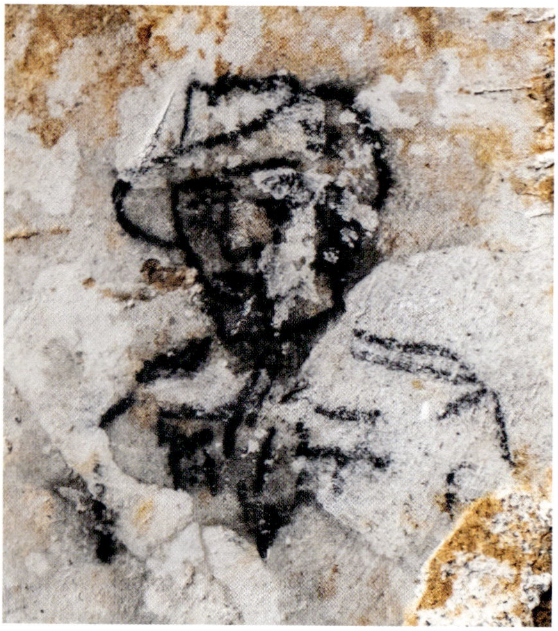

Left: A portrait of a 'Digger,' slang for soldiers from Australia and New Zealand, at Naours.

Below left: The inscription of Leslie Russell Blake at Naours.

Below right: Blake joined up in 1915. (Australian War Memorial)

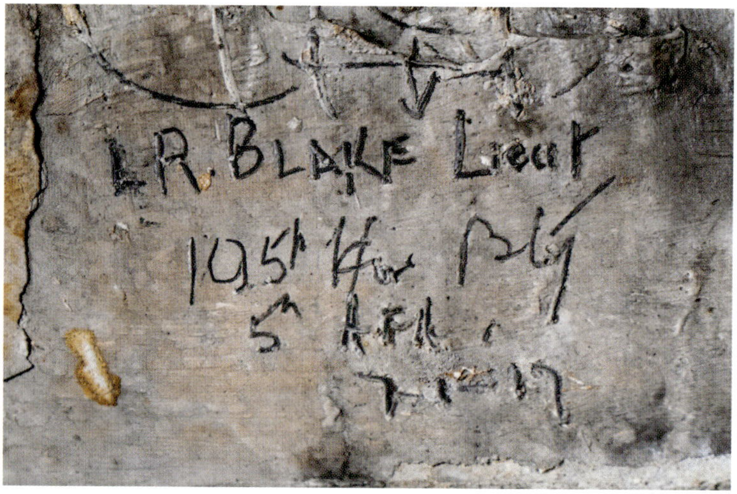

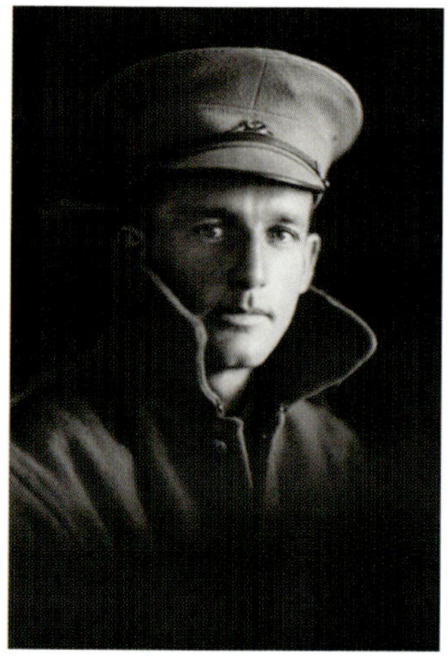

advance to take the German stronghold. When he returned, his flesh wound to the buttocks drew predictable taunts from his mates ('kept your head down but forgot about your arse'). But his feat won him recognition. The *London Gazette*, the official journal of record of the British government, contained an account of the 'conspicuous gallantry in action' that won him the Military Cross.

Before the war, from 1911 until 1914, Blake was a member of Mawson's Australasian Antarctic Expedition (AAE) to explore a long stretch of Antarctic coastline. He spent two years on Macquarie Island, halfway between New Zealand and Antarctica, as part of a five-man team tasked with relaying wireless communication between the expedition's

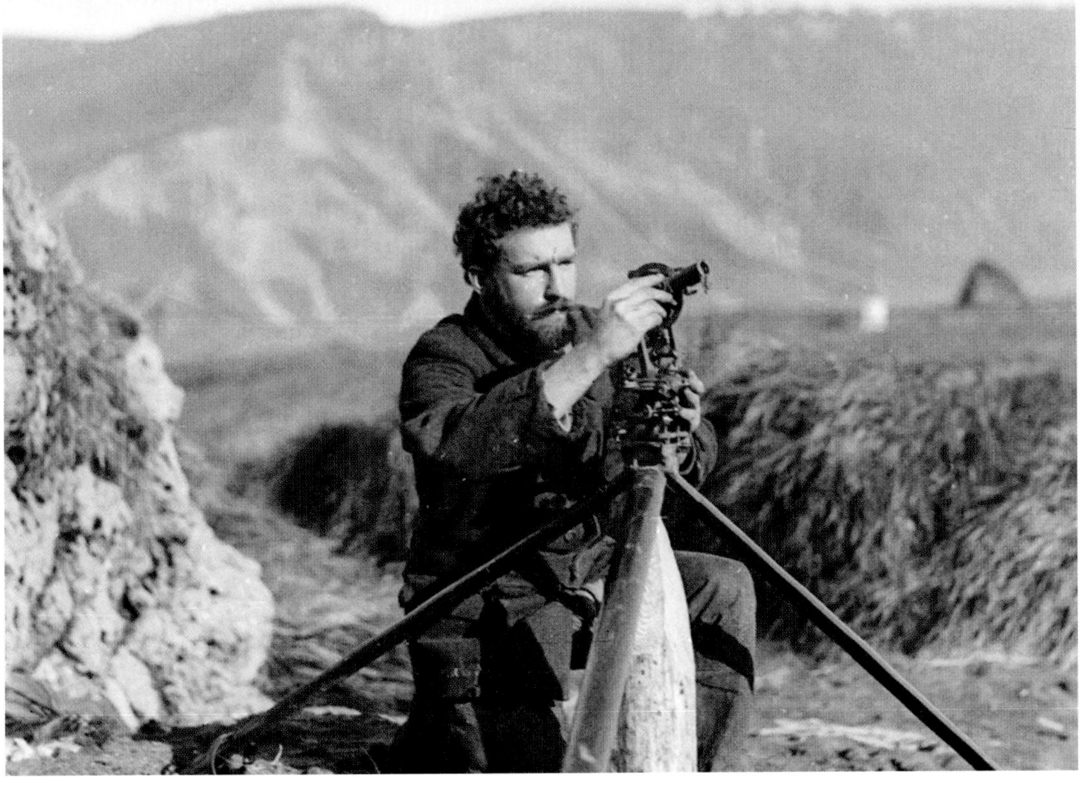

Blake surveying on Macquarie Island. (Mitchell Library, State Library of New South Wales)

main base on Commonwealth Bay in Antarctica, about 1,600 kilometres south-west of the island, to Sydney, 2,380 kilometres to the north-west. His job was to map and examine the geology of the island which is only 5 kilometres wide and 35 kilometres long but home to the world's entire royal penguin population during their annual breeding season. The map Blake produced was so accurate that it became the standard until it was superseded by modern techniques such as satellite imagery.

Meals included stuffed sea elephant's heart, and his team's ability to survive for two years on the island even though they had been provisioned for only one year, and to cope with violent weather swings, stood them in good stead for the privations of trench life.

In June 1917, when King George V presented the Military Cross to Blake in Buckingham Palace, he spotted the white ribbon of the Polar Medal, awarded to polar explorers, on Blake's tunic and asked him about it. They spoke for twenty minutes about Antarctica and the king became so engrossed in the conversation, keeping other medal recipients waiting, that Blake became worried he was going to miss a dental appointment. So, according to Blake family legend, he told the King of the United Kingdom and the British Dominions and Emperor of India: 'You will have to excuse me Your Majesty, but I have an urgent dental appointment on the other side of town.'

He sent the Military Cross to his fiancée in Australia, Frances Eileen Elliott. 'Was decorated by the King when over there,' he wrote to his older brother Will (William Henry Blake), when back in France at the end of June 1917, according to a biography of Blake by the biologist Herbert J.G. Dartnall. 'A lot of rot but still necessary.'

By that time he had spent six months attached to the headquarters of his division as a staff reconnaissance officer, which had taken him away from his comrades in the 105th Howitzer Battery – and from danger. 'I chucked the Staff job as I got fed up with it,' he wrote to Will on 26 July 1917 from Belgium. 'I've got a nice contract on in a few days – a hop over the bags with the infantry. If I get through it alright it ought to be a good stunt. If I don't it probably means a wooden cross.' His job was forward observation for the artillery – advancing with the infantry to report on the fall of Allied shells. The 'stunt' was the Third Battle of Ypres, the hundred-day mud-mired campaign to break out of the Ypres Salient, the bulge in the front line protruding into German-held territory east of the devastated Belgian city. Blake was seriously wounded when a 1½-inch fragment from a high-explosive shell sliced through his right forearm. He was sent to London for treatment, returned to his unit in early 1918 and was promoted to captain in May.

On the Western Front, the war raged along a relatively narrow 650-kilometre strip from the North Sea to the Swiss border. But when on leave from the shell-pocked landscapes of devastated villages and stinking trenches, soldiers found themselves in what must have been a mind-boggling parallel world of calm and colour. On 21 September 1918, Blake wrote that he had just returned from a two-week holiday in the south of France. 'Nice, Menton, Monte Carlo, Cannes and Mentone – some place,' he wrote. 'I can assure you one may as well see the world at the expense of the Army when it is possible – don't you think so old man? There is plenty of sun there like Australia and the scenery is glorious. They have planted Blue Gums, Moreton Bay Figs, River Oak, Currajong and about 6 different kinds of wattle - so it makes it something like home.'

The war was nearly over. Blake had been fighting in France and Belgium for two and a half years. Less than a month later, at dusk on 2 October 1918, during the Hundred Days Offensive of Allied advances in which the AIF played a major part, Blake was on horseback near the French village of Hargicourt, supervising the unloading of ammunition. Suddenly, a stray artillery shell exploded under his horse, killing the animal, blowing off part of his left leg, fracturing his skull and wounding his face and thigh. Still alive, he was taken to a casualty clearing station. He was operated on, but died on the morning of the next day, 3 October, thirty-nine days before the Armistice.

Lieutenant Charles Morton, who enlisted with Blake in 1915 and who saw him almost as a brother, wrote to Will about Blake's final hours.

'I was beside him when he was severely wounded, dressed the wounds myself and helped to carry him to a place of safety,' Morton wrote, according to Dartnall's biography. 'His left leg had gone and his head had also been much mutilated but he was quite conscious right up to the time he was operated at the C.C.S. (casualty clearing station). We heard subsequently that he had passed away quietly at 6am the following morning that would be on 3/10/18. His memory will ever live in all those who knew him for his undoubted bravery, his fairness and his ability. He had a mind of his own and was never afraid to speak it.'

The writing on the wall in Naours wasn't the only scribbled trace of Leslie Russell Blake to be discovered by chance.

In 2001, Dr Martyn L. Gorman, a zoologist at the University of Aberdeen, was exploring the contents of a dusty cupboard in the university's Zoology Museum when he came across a penguin egg. Written on it in black ink were the initials L.R.B and the date 20.10.12. Dr Gorman soon found out that the egg had been collected by Leslie Russell Blake during the Antarctic expedition. He believes it may have been brought to Aberdeen by a biologist who had worked at the Mawson Institute for Antarctic Research in Adelaide.

Dr Gorman decided to find out more the talented geologist and brave soldier whose life took him from the windswept wastes of the Antarctic to the blood-soaked mud of the Western Front. Moved by what he learned, he visited Tincourt New British Cemetery in 2004, just a few miles down the road from where Blake fell, and on a late summer evening laid a poppy on his grave.

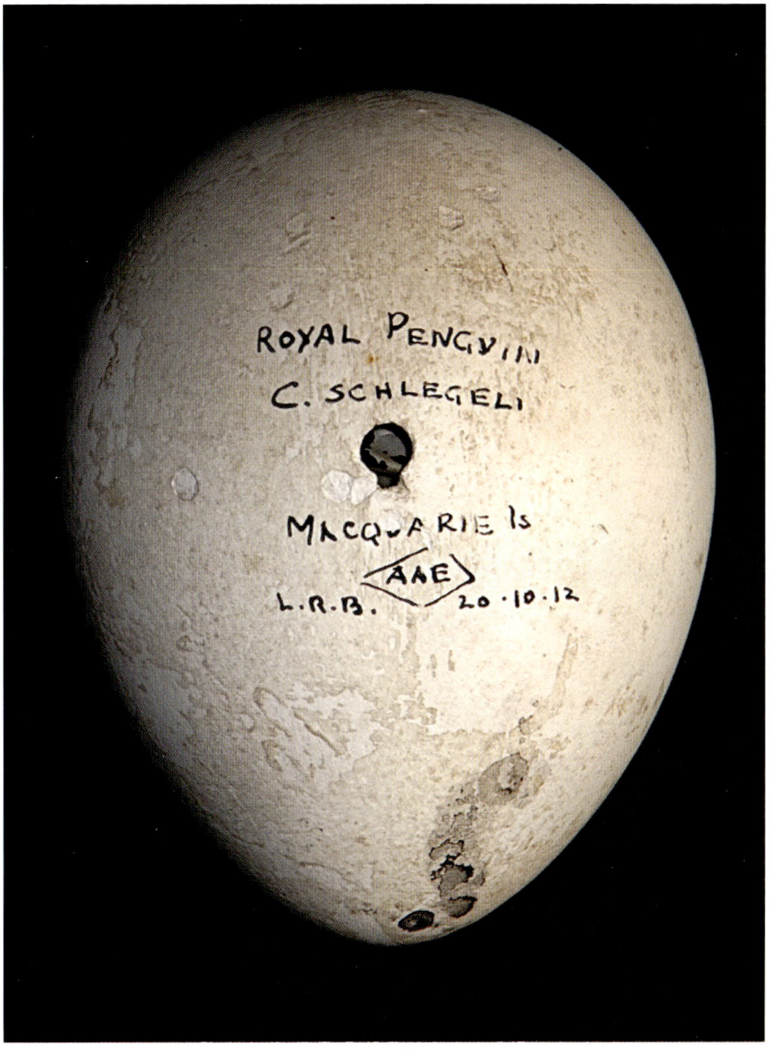

Blake's royal penguin egg. (Photograph by Dr Martyn L. Gorman, University of Aberdeen Zoology Museum)

The Modest VC

'Sgt. S. Meekosha V. C. 46th West Yorks.' The inscription discovered in 2015 is among the comparatively few that were made by British troops in Naours. It is not known when Meekosha visited the caves, but it was after he won the Victoria Cross that turned the soldier, described as modest and private, into a celebrity.

On 19 November 1915, then-Corporal Samuel Meekosha of the 1/6th Battalion, West Yorkshire Regiment, Territorial Force, was in a trench near the Yser Canal 2 miles north-north-east of Ypres. It was cold and wet, and the Germans kept sending over 'whizz-bangs,' light, high-velocity shells that were feared because they arrived with virtually no warning, as well as heavy shells. The war diary for the battalion states in hand-written pencil: 'One of our Companies heavily shelled by enemy, six being killed and seven wounded. Enemy were very active all day, shelling our positions with heavy shells. Retaliation was called for and obtained from artillery.' Those dry words masked the drama of the day. The *London Gazette* of 22 January 1916 described the 'most conspicuous' bravery shown by Corporal Samuel Meekosha. It wrote:

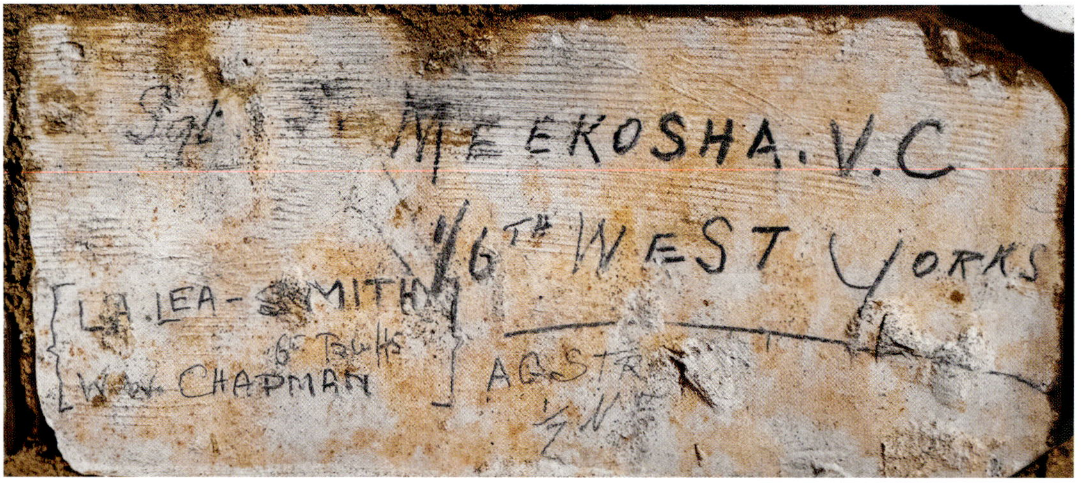

Meekosha's inscription at Naours.

> He was with a platoon of about 20 Non-Commissioned Officers and men, who were holding an isolated trench. During a very heavy bombardment by the enemy six of the platoon were killed and seven wounded, while all the remainder were more or less buried. When the senior Non-Commissioned Officers had been either killed or wounded Corporal Meekosha at once took command, sent a runner for assistance, and, in spite of no less than 10 more big shells falling within 20 yards of him, continued to dig out the wounded and buried men in full view of the enemy and at close range from the German trenches. By his promptness and magnificent courage and determination he saved at least four lives.

The twenty-two-year-old had enlisted in the Territorial Force in February 1911 and was mobilised on 5 August 1914, a day after Britain declared war on Germany.

He was awarded the Victoria Cross by King George V at Buckingham Palace on 4 March 1916 and featured on the front page of the *Daily Mirror*. The newspaper of his hometown, the *Bradford Weekly Telegraph*, also devoted a front-page story to him headlined 'The Bradford Man of the Week.' A week later, *The Times* reported that Meekosha had been entertained to luncheon by the Lord Mayor of Bradford, Thomas Howarth. 'Replying to the Lord Mayor, Meekosha said he had only done what had been done by many others and what many others would do,' the report said. He also featured in a Gallaher cigarette

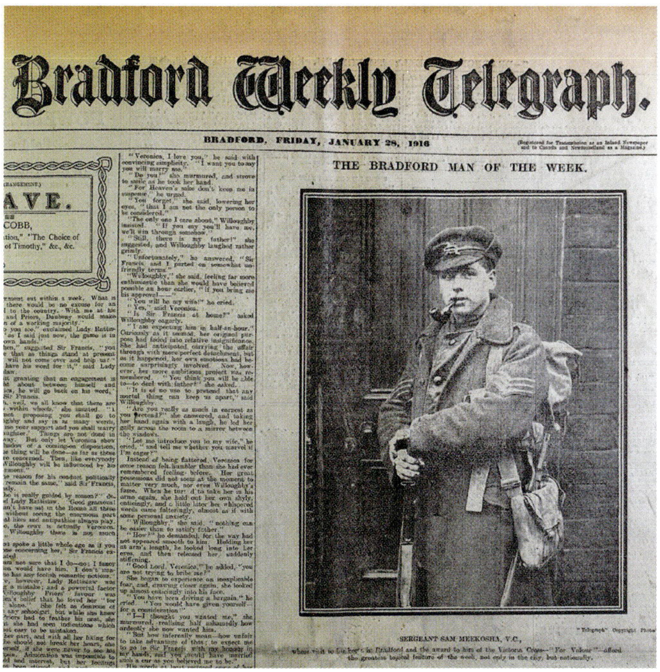

Bradford Weekly Telegraph.

BRADFORD, FRIDAY, JANUARY 28, 1916

THE BRADFORD MAN OF THE WEEK.

SERGEANT SAM MEEKOSHA, V.C.

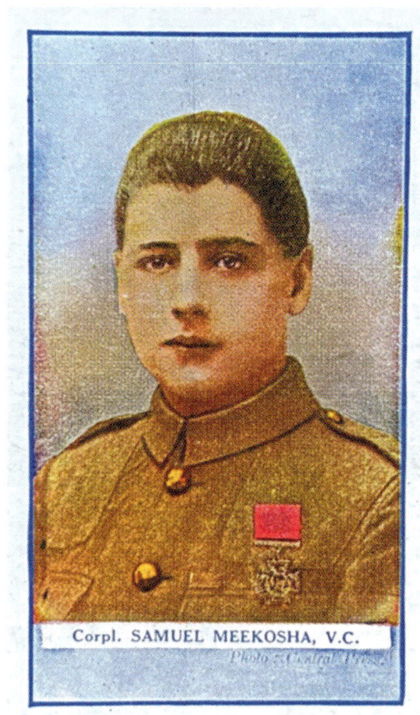

Above left: Meekosha on the front page of his home town's newspaper. (Courtesy of the *Telegraph & Argus* newspaper, Bradford)

Above right: Cigarette card featuring Samuel Meekosha, one of a series of cards on Victoria Cross winners. (Courtesy of Meekosha's great-niece, Sandra Montgomery)

card collection of 'Victoria Cross Heroes.' Meekosha died in 1950, aged fifty-seven. In 2001, his name made headlines again when his VC medal was sold by his granddaughter at Sotheby's to an anonymous private collector for over £101,200.

Meekosha, Blake and Edmonds are among 500 soldiers Prilaux and his team have identified so far from the inscriptions in Naours. A total of 3,200 have been logged here, of which 2,200 are Australian.

The graffiti was made by men who came here to be distracted for a few hours from the war, who wanted to leave a trace of themselves as individuals but who also identified with the military units they invariably cited. They were proud to be soldiers. Each name stands for a story.

Alister Ross emigrated from Scotland to Australia in 1912 at the age of nineteen with a pocket Bible given to him by his mother, Annie Maria. The creamery worker, one of four brothers who served in the war, joined the 9th Battalion of the Australian Imperial Force in January 1915 and arrived in Gallipoli in June. During an action there, that Bible saved his life when two pieces of shrapnel penetrated the book from Revelations through to Judges. He was then sent to the Somme, where he fought in the battalion that captured Pozières. He pressed flowers from Gallipoli and poppies from the Somme in the Bible and wrote on the pages. On his twenty-second birthday, 6 August 1916, shortly after being promoted to corporal, he wrote on the inside cover: 'Came safely through the battle of Pozieres. Battle lasted nearly a week. My battalion had many casualties. I had many narrow escapes. Came through safely.'

Just over two weeks later, on the night of 21 August in an attack on a German stronghold at Mouquet Farm, he was wounded but refused to retire and was then buried by a collapsing trench under severe shellfire, according to his nephew Ross Fuller. He was dug out but did not

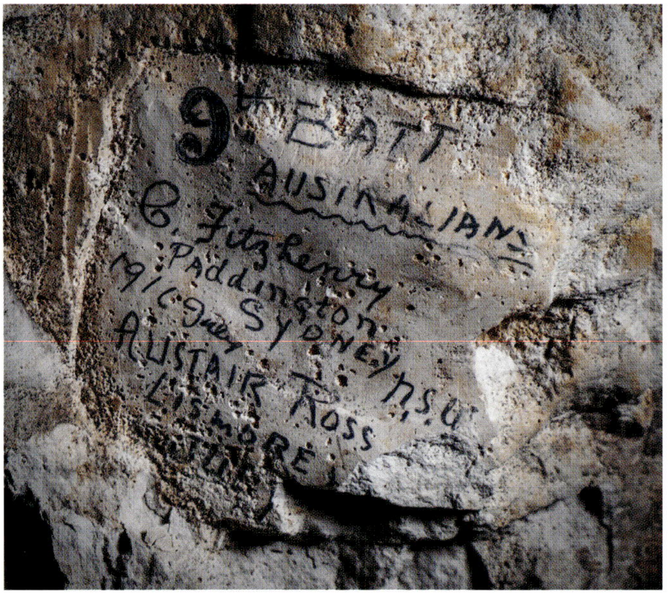

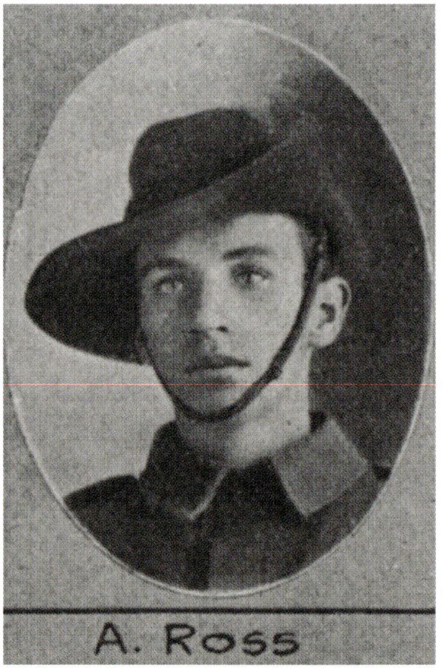

Above left: Alister Ross's inscription at Naours.

Above right: Alister Ross. (Courtesy of his nephew Ross Fuller)

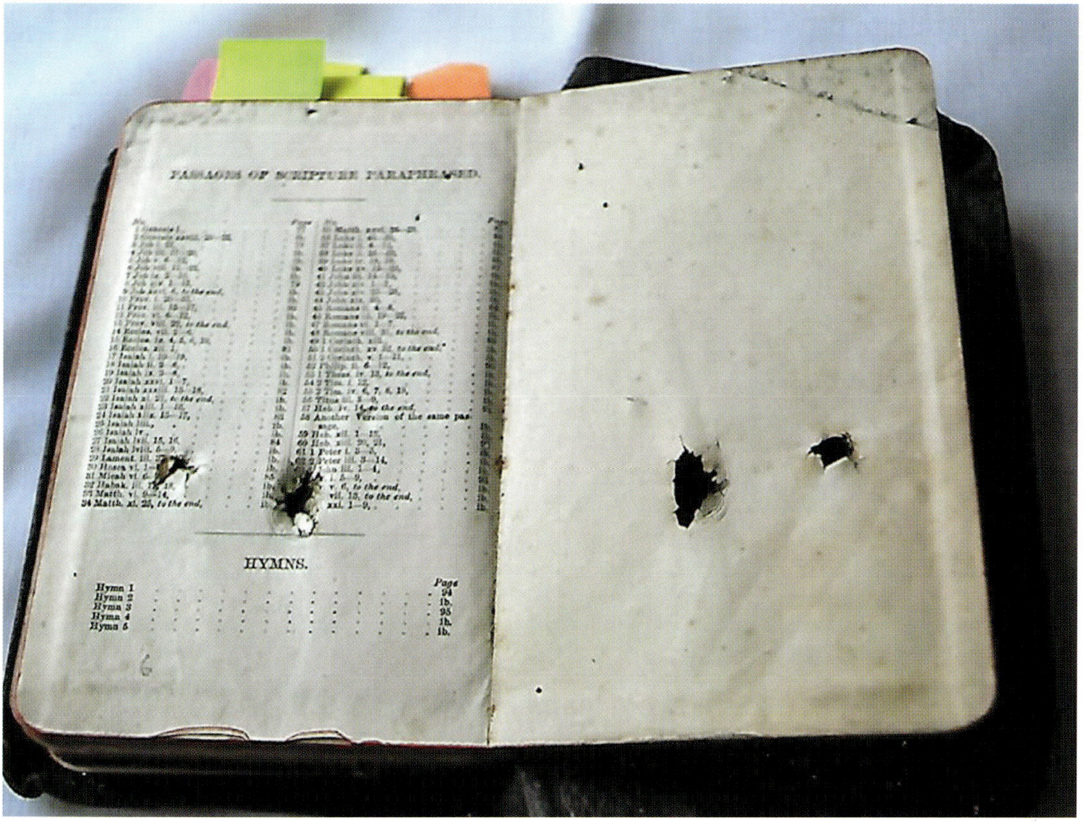

Alister Ross's shrapnel-pierced Bible. (Courtesy of Ross Fuller)

survive and was buried behind the lines. Alister's body was never recovered. His name is on the Villers-Bretonneux War Memorial for those Australians with no known grave. His Bible made it back to his family. In 2018, they donated it to the Anzac Memorial Museum in Sydney.

Harold Raymond George Edwards is also among the names in Naours. The mechanic in the 3rd Squadron of the Australian Flying Corps was a watchmaker by trade and came from Bendigo in the state of Victoria. He became an instrument fitter for British-made RE8 reconnaissance biplanes, and on 21 and 22 April 1918 stood guard over the body of German flying ace Manfred von Richthofen, the Red Baron, who had been shot down by Allied forces. In an interview he gave the author Adrian Hellwig in 1990 aged ninety-four, Edwards recalled the excitement surrounding the Red Baron's death and that there were 'lots of bigwigs popping in.' But he didn't think quite as much of the Red Baron as many others.

> I understood that he would get up early before light and get an umbrella of other chaps all around him, eight or ten chaps (the Circus they called it) and then if they saw something they just all hopped down and when the poor sod they'd caught didn't have a chance, Richthofen had the pleasure of shooting him down. I didn't look on that as being the wonderful dog-fighter he was credited as being.

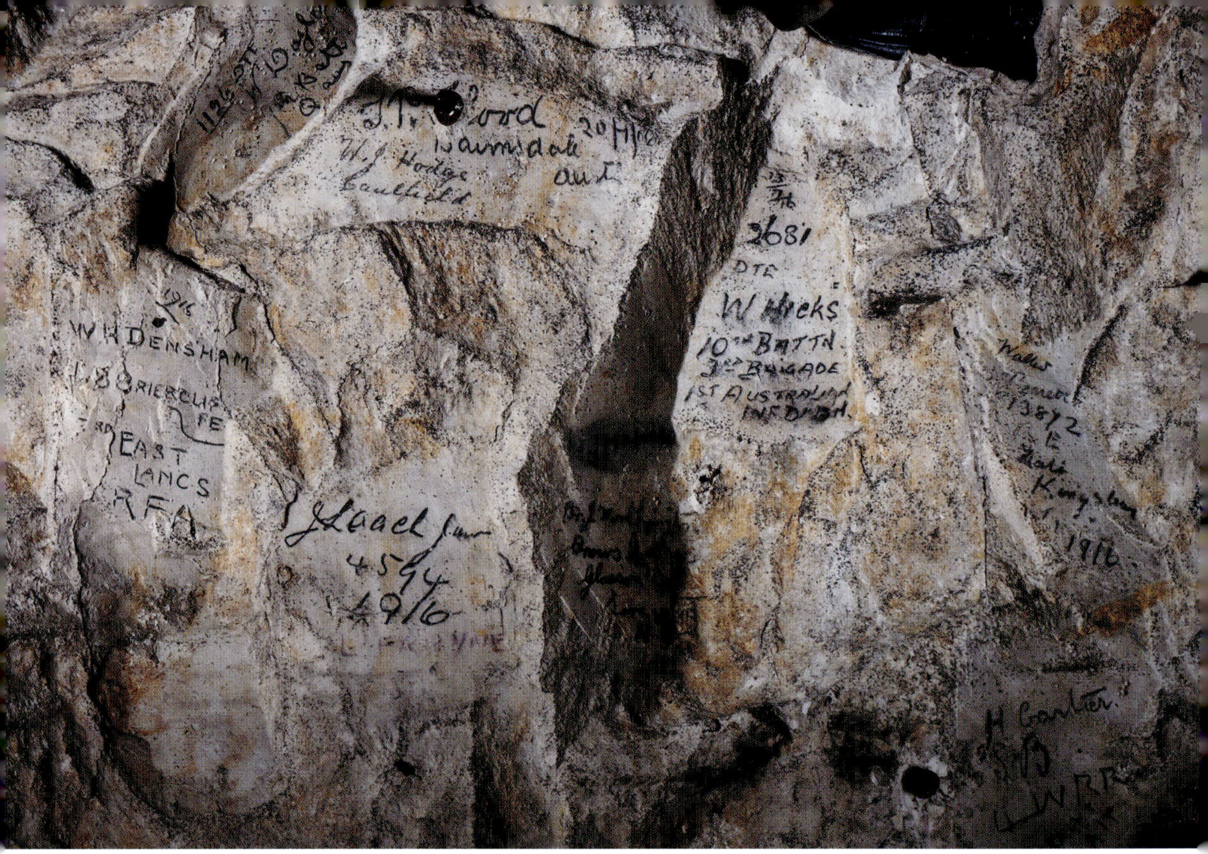

Above: Pencil inscriptions at Naours. On the left, Walter Henry Densham of the Royal Field Artillery, died on 5 April 1918 at the age of nineteen. He was a lieutenant and had won the Military Cross. Louis Bernard Briercliffe died on 31 March 1917, a second lieutenant, aged twenty-seven. They both served in the Royal Field Artillery, East Lancashire Brigade.

Below: A tunnel at Naours.

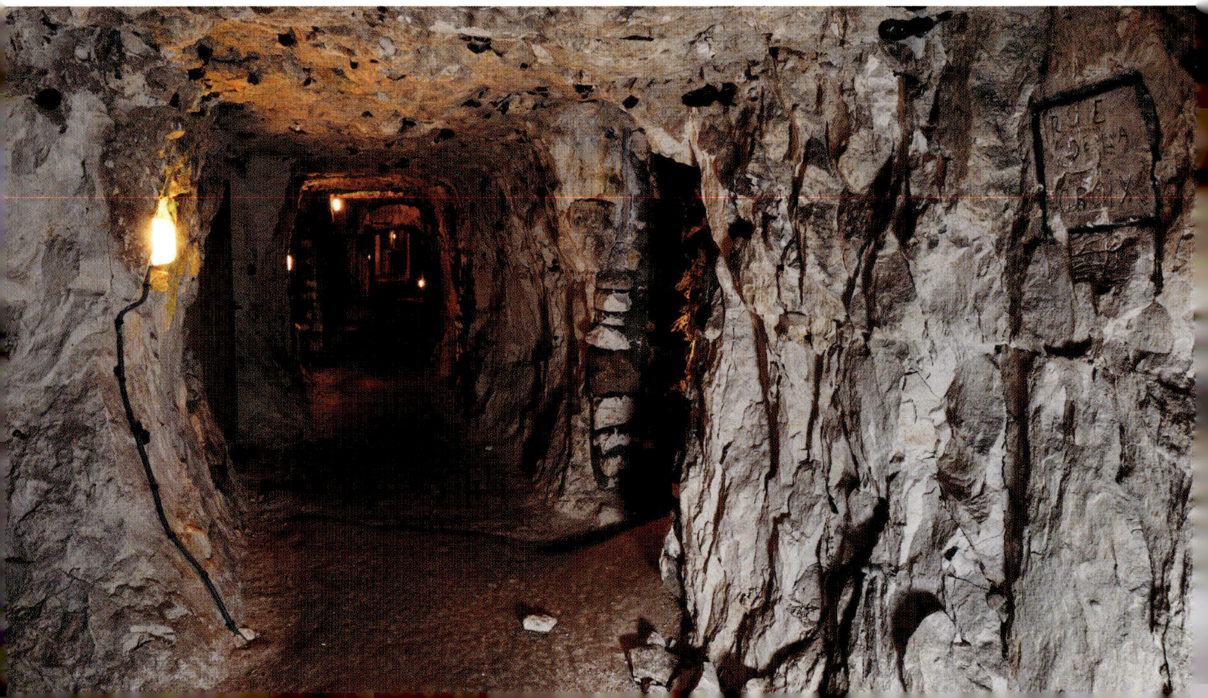

Edwards was also tasked with engraving the plaques for the Red Baron's cross and coffin. As he did so, he couldn't help thinking 'I wish they'd got him sooner,' he recalled. Described as 'sharp as a tack' into old age, Edwards lived to 102, passing away in Brisbane in 1998.

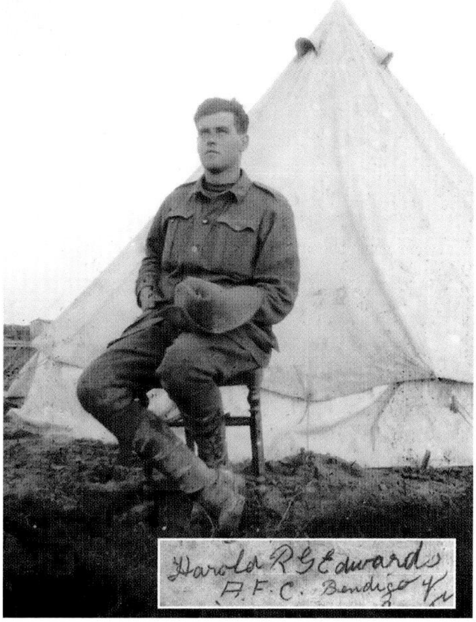

Right: Harold Raymond George Edwards, a mechanic in the 3rd Squadron of the Australian Flying Corps. (Courtesy of Adrian Hellwig). The inset photo shows Edwards' inscription at Naours.

Below: All the honours: the funeral of Manfred von Richthofen at Bertangles in April 1918. He now lies buried in Wiesbaden. (La Contemporaine VAL 413/127 Producer: British official photo)

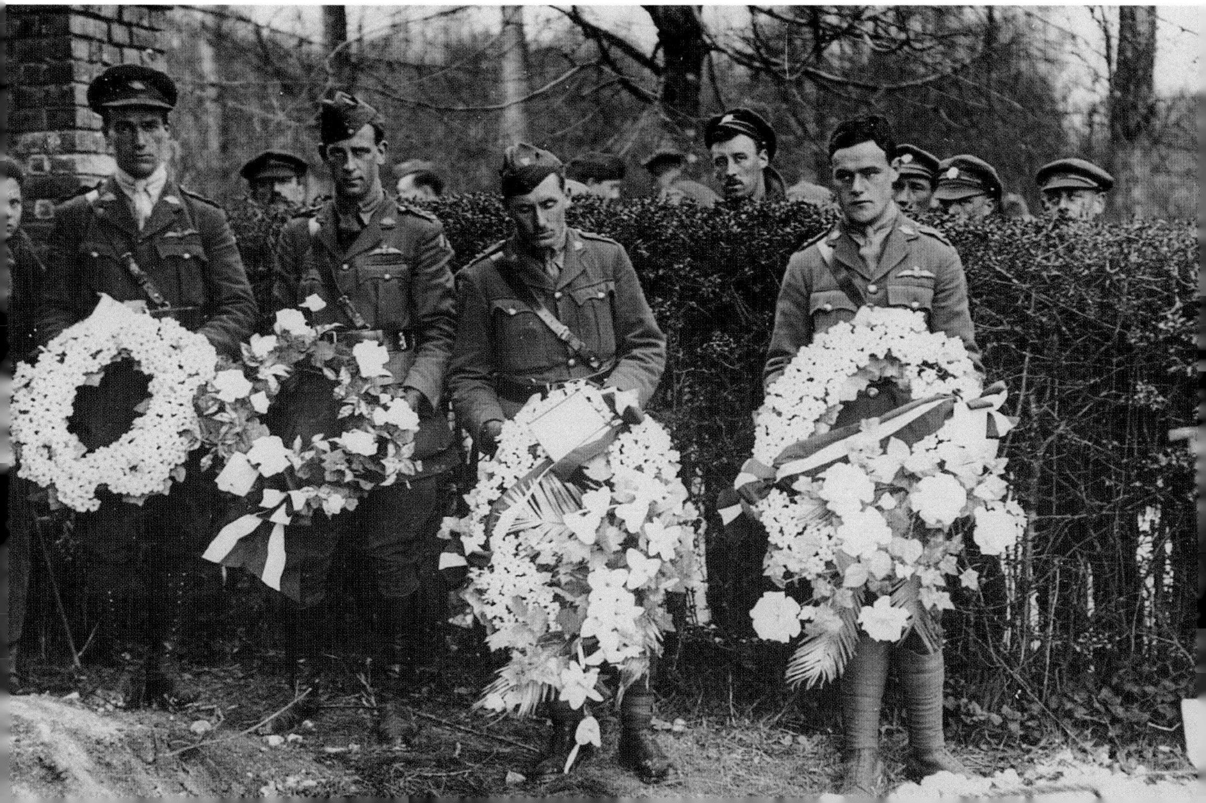

The Final Hours

Private Aleck James Ambler of the 13th Battalion (Royal Highland Regiment) was born in England and emigrated to Canada in 1905. He was a stonecutter by trade and put those skills to use ahead of the Battle of Vimy Ridge in April 1917 by creating some of the finest carvings yet found under the Western Front.

His works adorn the walls of the Maison Blanche limestone quarry north of Arras where hundreds of men sheltered in the weeks leading up to the assault that became a defining moment in Canadian history.

Among Ambler's creations were the insignia of his regiment, the Royal Highlanders of Canada, alongside a panel with the regiment's battle honours, which included the Second Battle of Ypres and the Somme. He signed that carving 'PTE A.J. Ambler' and gave his service number, '887386', and the date, 'MAR 7, 17'.

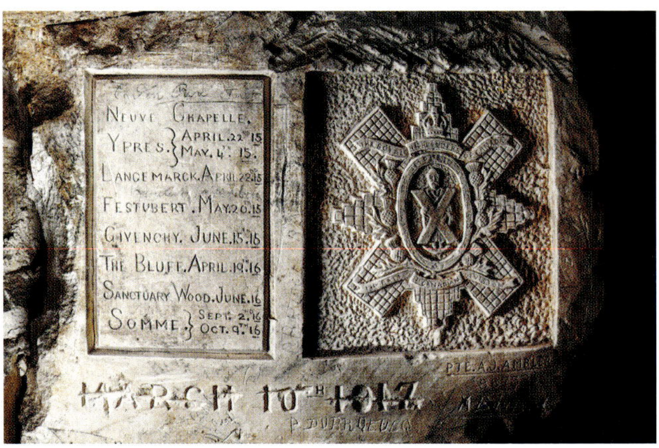

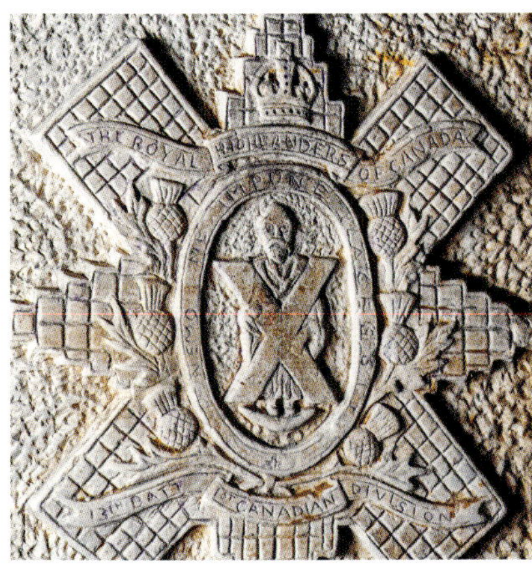

Above left: Aleck Ambler's works include the regimental badge of the Royal Highlanders of Canada, alongside its battle honours including the Second Battle of Ypres and the Somme.

Above right: This close-up shows the intricacy and skill of Ambler's work. The figure is St Andrew, the patron saint of Scotland.

Three works have been ascribed to Ambler among the more than 1,000 carvings, drawings and inscriptions made almost exclusively by members of the Canadian Expeditionary Force between late 1916 and the spring of 1917.

He was thirty-two, married and the father of a two-year-old boy. He was a sniper, tasked with killing enemy snipers and taking out trench periscopes and other observation devices. He survived the assault on the ridge but was seriously wounded on 5 June when a piece of shrapnel severed his Achilles tendon and put him out of the war.

According to his service file, Ambler's wound became infected and he suffered from gas gangrene, a common and often fatal affliction for wounded soldiers in the field. Their uniforms were caked in churned-up mud that had for years been fertilised with horse manure, and when struck by bullets or shrapnel, parts of their uniform would become lodged in their wounds, causing gaseous swelling and intense pain.

Ambler had muscle tissue removed from his left calf and it took months for the wound to heal. 'Walks on left toes,' his medical record states. 'Heel raised about 6 inches.'

He was treated in hospitals in England from July 1917 to March 1918 when he was invalided to Canada. Discharged from the army on medical grounds with a permanent walking disability, he didn't lose his artistic streak, decorating cakes and raffling them to raise money for the Boy Scouts. He died in 1974 at the age of eighty-nine.

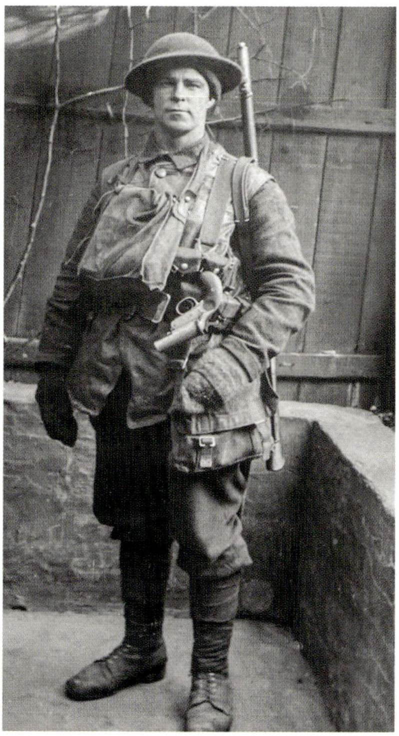

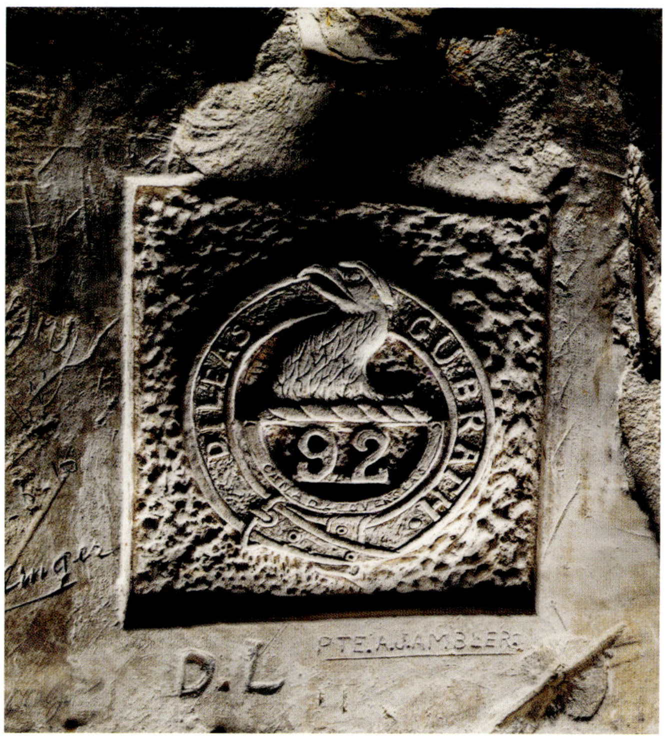

Above left: Aleck Ambler in France, 24 January 1917. (Courtesy of his grandson, Mike Ambler)

Above right: Another of Ambler's works: the cap badge of the Canadian 92nd Infantry Battalion. (48th Highlanders)

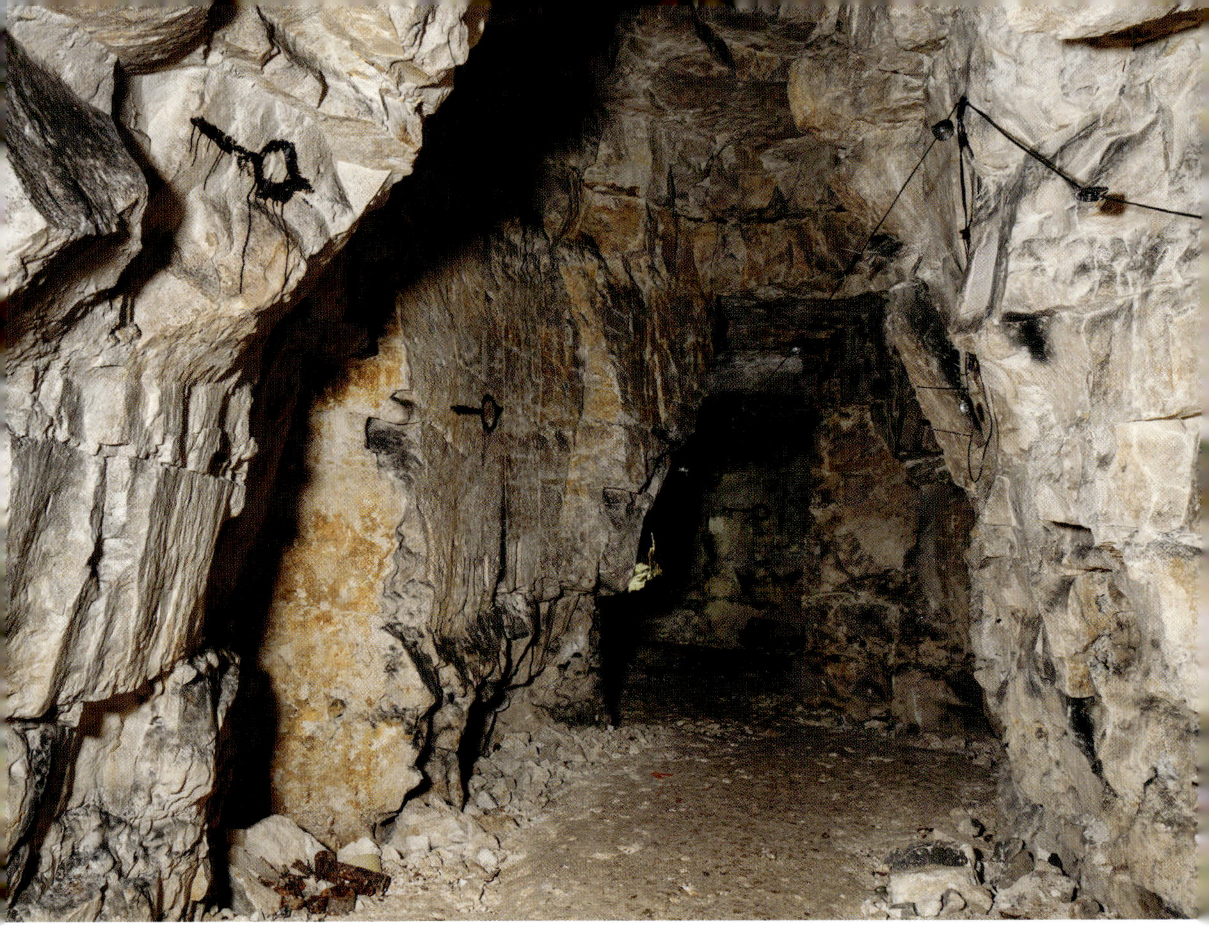

The original arrows painted by Thomas Cook guides in the inter-war years can still be seen in the Maison Blanche quarry.

Maison Blanche became a tourist attraction in the inter-war years as veterans and their families visited the site on battlefield tours. Arrows roughly daubed on the walls by Thomas Cook guides to direct visitors are still visible today.

After the Second World War, farmers used the quarry as a rubbish dump. It lay forgotten for half a century until it was rediscovered by the local historian Dominique Faivre and later cleared and surveyed by members of the Durand Group, a British-based voluntary organisation that explores the subterranean landscapes of the Western Front. Made up of experts in bomb disposal, tunnelling and archaeology, the organisation takes its name from the 6,000-pound British Durand mine that lies under a public area of the Vimy Ridge memorial park and was made safe by group members in 1998.

Private Ambler's son Aleck was overwhelmed when he came face to face with his work for the first time in 2007 during a visit organised by the Canadian documentary company YAP Films. He said: 'What amazes me is that he never talked about it. He just said, "I carved some badges in the trenches" and he wasn't too sure whether he put his name on all of them or not.'

Running his fingers over one of the carvings, Aleck said: 'This makes me feel so much closer to him, close enough that I could go in the next room and he would be there. I could just go in there and sit down and talk to him.'

In an environment of blood and iron where art counted for nothing, the carvings in Maison Blanche crafted by battle-hardened men who knew exactly what they were about to face are astoundingly life-affirming.

David Hedges, a member of the Durand Group, estimates that it took Ambler 40 hours to complete just one of his creations. That effort in itself is a message. 'No man will spend that much time carving the cap badge of his regiment if his morale is down,' said Hedges.

Maison Blanche is replete with carvings of the Canadian Maple Leaf symbol and regimental insignia of varying quality, some almost as fine as Ambler's. As they embellished the walls with their trench knives or doodled idly with their pencils whilst lying in their bunks stacked three high along the walls, the quarry trembled from German shell blasts that sent earth raining from the ceiling. The stagnant air was thick with dust, the smell of food and the odours of men – Maison Blanche could shelter more than 200 at any one time.

The men knew that every minute mattered.

'Most of the graffiti was made just before the Vimy Ridge assault in April 1917 and for a lot of soldiers these inscriptions were the last trace of them because they were killed in the battle,' said Faivre, who found the trove in 2001 after wriggling over rubbish clogging the entrance and who drew public attention to the carvings. He has identified more than 400 soldiers who immortalised themselves in the quarry.

Two soldiers from the 15th Canadian Infantry Battalion, Thomas Mason and William Percy Beckett, created an enduring testament to their skill by carving what they called a *FRANCE 1917 LETTER BOX* into the wall, signed and dated 16 March 1917.

The cap badge of the 16th Infantry Battalion (Canadian Scottish) formed from four companies of Highland regiments in Canada. The Gaelic motto *Deas gu cath* means 'Ready for the fray'.

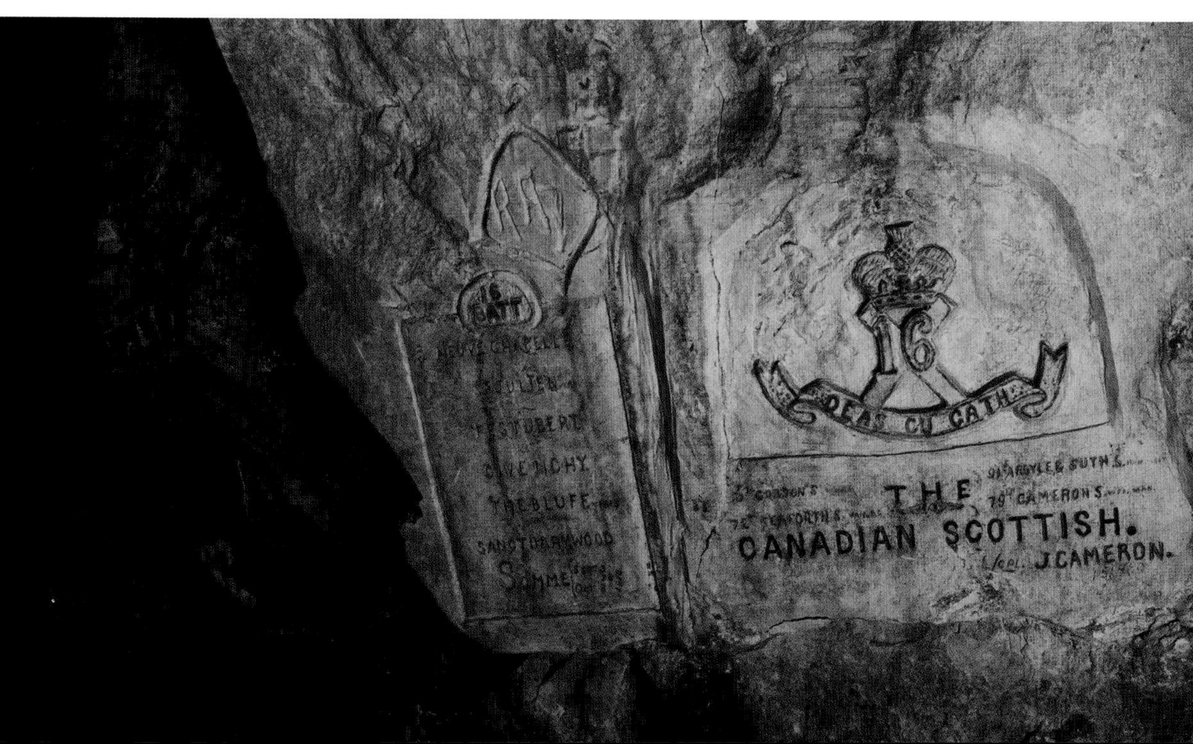

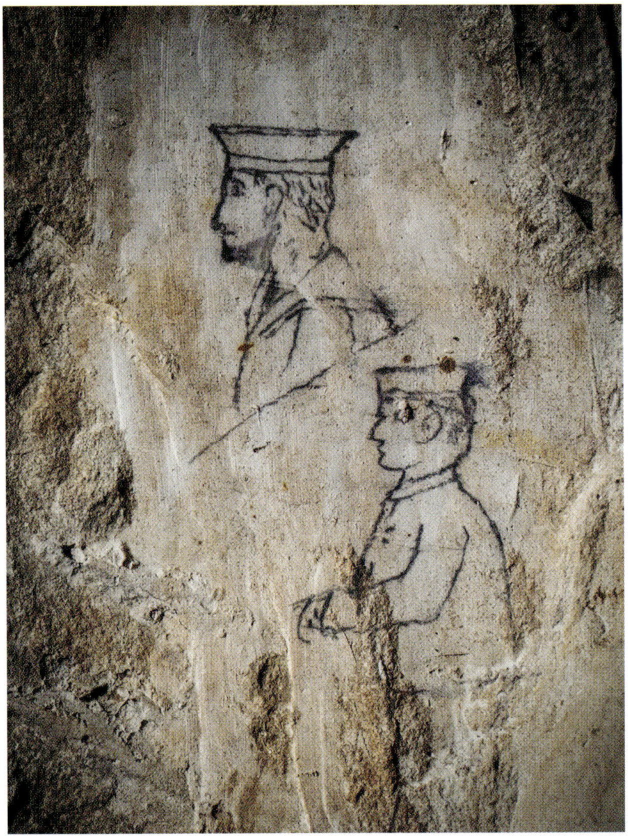

Left: A drawing believed to be of a Canadian navy seaman (top) and a German seaman (bottom).

Below: The 'France 1917 Letter Box' carved by Thomas Mason and William Percy Beckett. Both were wounded in the 9 April attack on Vimy Ridge.

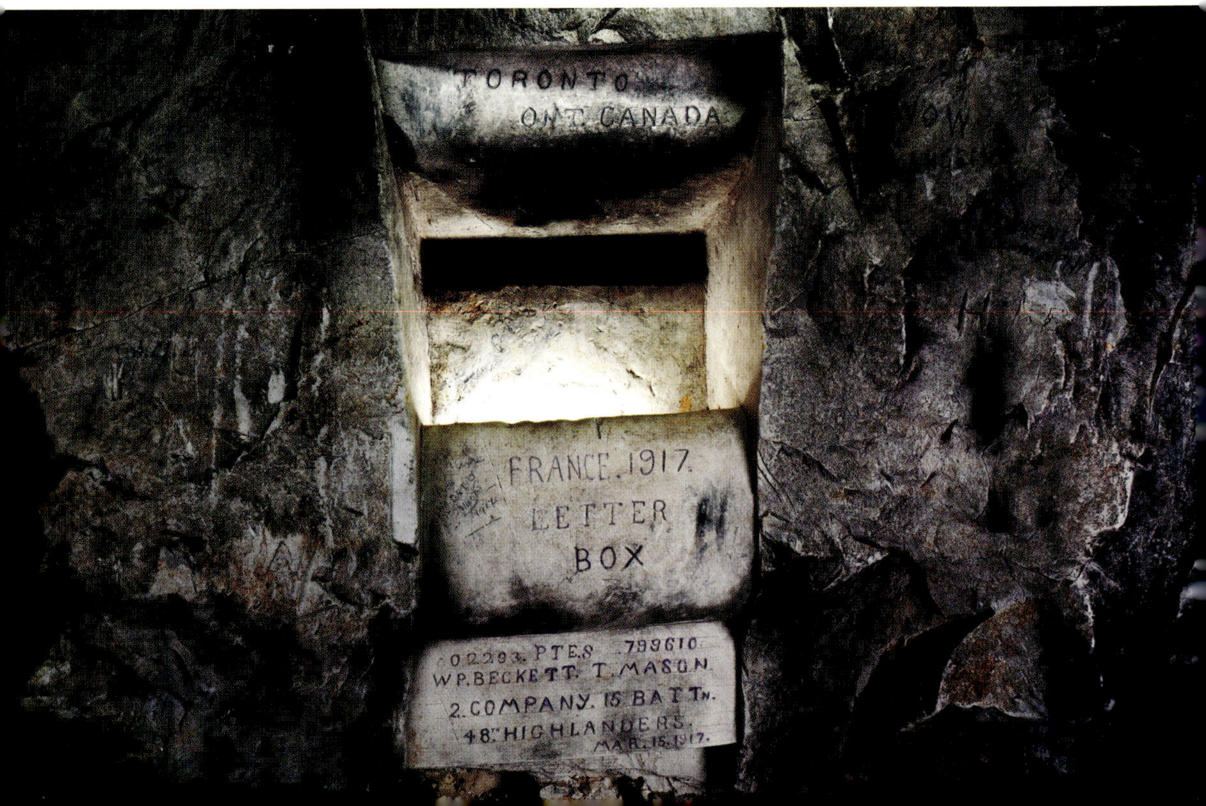

Like so many men in the Canadian Expeditionary Force, they were born in England and were among the more than one million immigrants from Britain and Ireland who sought a better life in Canada in the early 1900s up until the outbreak of war.

Both took part in the 9 April attack on Vimy Ridge, in which over 10,000 Canadian troops were killed or wounded, and both were wounded on that day. Private Mason was hit in the right hand either by a piece of shrapnel or an 'explosive bullet' – both causes are cited in his army medical records. He had to have his little finger amputated. 'Power of the grip of right hand 50% of that of left hand,' a doctor noted. That, together with flat feet he had developed in France, got him discharged in August 1918 as 'unfit for further service overseas and not needed for duty in Canada.' He died in 1970 at the age of eighty-one.

Private William Percy Beckett, a farm labourer, received a gunshot wound to the left arm. He recovered in Britain and didn't return to France until April 1918. He rejoined his unit, the 15th Battalion, in the field on 7 September, and also survived the war.

The wounds they suffered would probably have prevented them from crafting a work like their Letter Box ever again. Over a century on, their still-pristine creation, hewn clean and smooth out of the jagged limestone, stands as a 'memorial to their pre-battle unwounded selves,' the archaeologist Matthew Leonard wrote.

As one walks along the passages, it is the carvings that immediately catch the eye. But the pencil writings and drawings tell their own powerful stories.

Lying on one of the bunk beds long since removed, no doubt wondering whether he would see his faraway home and his parents, seven sisters and brother ever again, Earl Leroy Lacey, a farm boy from Dunwich, Ontario, drew a pig with a pronounced corkscrew tail, a horse and a chicken.

Lacey survived the battle. His battalion remained in the thick of it that year in fighting at Arleux, the Scarpe river, Loos and in the mud of Passchendaele. On 18 August, he was granted ten days' leave in England, and again on 24 November.

On 23 February 1918, he was out on patrol at Hill 70 near Lens when he was hit in the head by an enemy machine gun bullet and died shortly afterwards.

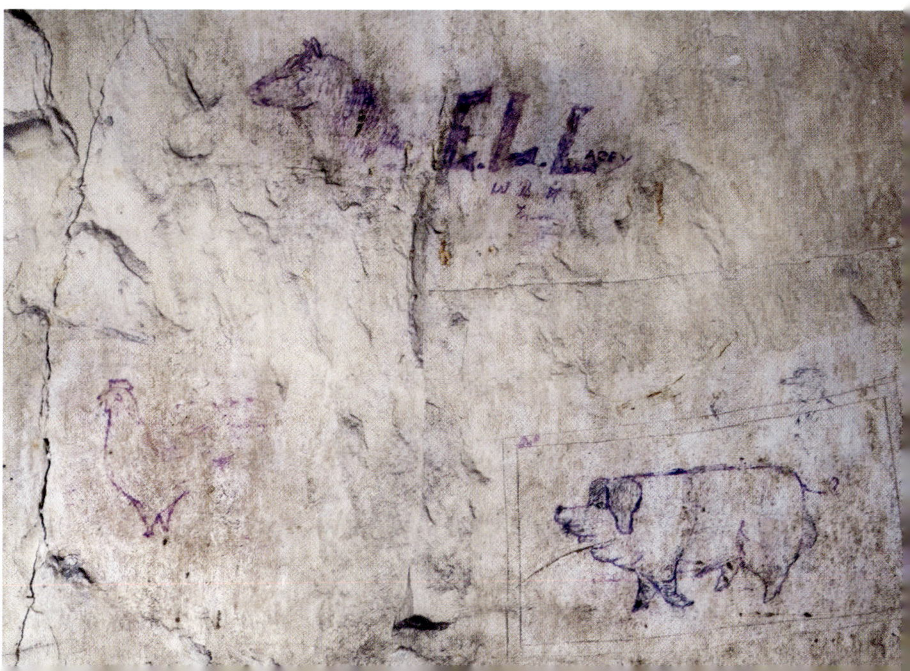

The farm animals drawn by Private Earl Leroy Lacey.

He lies buried in Aix-Noulette Communal Cemetery Extension. His drawings, gradually fading in the dampness of the quarry, still ring with his longing for home and a life in peace.

On the opposite wall, a small smooth rectangle frames the names of the brothers William Thomas Harvey and Clarence Otto Harvey along with their hometown of McKellar, Ontario. They worked on the family farm with their mother and two brothers.

William was the older, at twenty-three, and had gained military experience in a militia before he and Clarence, nineteen, joined up on the same day, 11 March 1916, in the small town of Parry Sound in south-eastern Canada. When they arrived in Liverpool on 11 November 1916, their 162nd Battalion was disbanded and its members sent to reinforce units depleted in earlier battles. Both were transferred to the 35th Battalion but William was promoted to sergeant shortly afterwards. In a sign that he wanted to stay close to his younger brother, he asked to be demoted back to private.

They arrived in France on 27 February 1917. Their inscription in Maison Blanche isn't dated but, in uneven typing, the war diary of their battalion notes that on 30 March, the unit 'relieved 16th Canadian Battalion in Brigade Support at MAISON BLANCHE.'

It is likely that on that night, or on 31 March or 1 April, the two brothers, successful so far in staying together, wrote their inscription. On the night of 1 April, the battalion was redeployed to nearby trenches in the Labyrinthe section - – the name given by the French to the maze of German trenches, dug-outs and machine-gun posts at the southern edge of

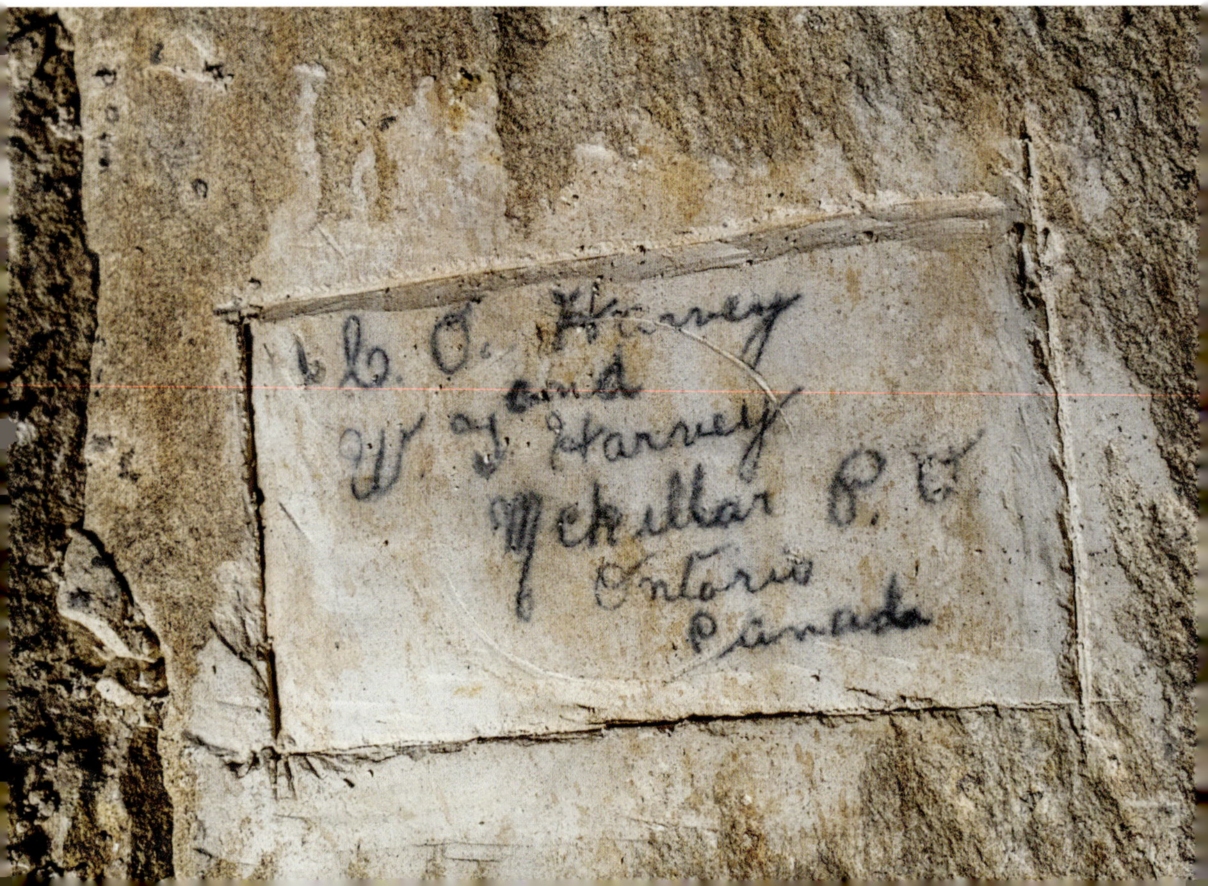

The Harvey brothers' inscription.

the 7.5-kilometre Vimy Ridge. After raids on German positions, the battalion marched on to rest billets at the village of Camblain-l'Abbé on 5 April.

The assault on the ridge on 9 April forced them apart. On that day, William was struck by a bullet, suffering a 'penetrating wound through upper part of right arm,' according to his medical record. He was evacuated to England. Clarence fought on, until 4 May 1917 when he was killed during the Canadian attack on the heavily fortified village of Fresnoy.

The news will have reached William while he was in a Canadian military hospital in Orpington, Kent, recovering from his infected wound. The death of his brother is said to have had a lasting impact on him. The convalescent home in Epsom where he stayed in July 1917 after receiving massage and physiotherapy for his stiff shoulder noted: 'Patient is nervous.'

He returned to France in November 1917 and ended the war as an ammunition driver. He returned to Canada in April 1919 and went back to the family farm. He died in 1975 aged eighty-two.

'The young men sheltering here knew that it was very difficult outside,' said Arnaud Durier, a medical doctor and local councillor committed to preserving the heritage of Maison Blanche. 'In here, for a few hours, they were free to think about their life, their farm, their loved-ones, and to carve or write what they felt. These walls tell of their hearts, their minds, and their fears.'

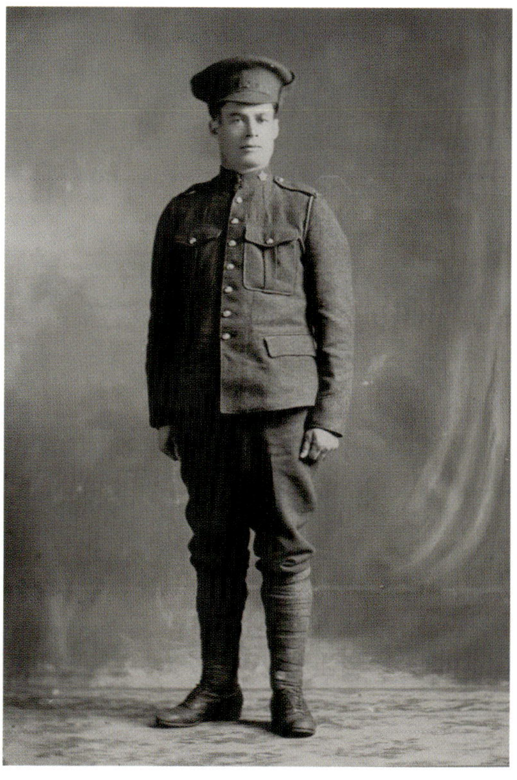

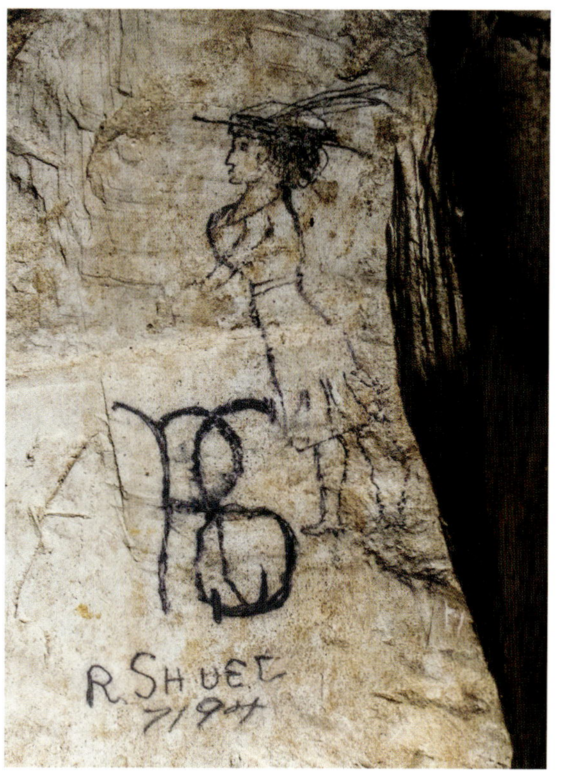

Above left: Clarence Otto Harvey, who was killed on 4 May 1917. (Courtesy of Dominique Faivre)

Above right: A drawing of a buxom woman in Maison Blanche.

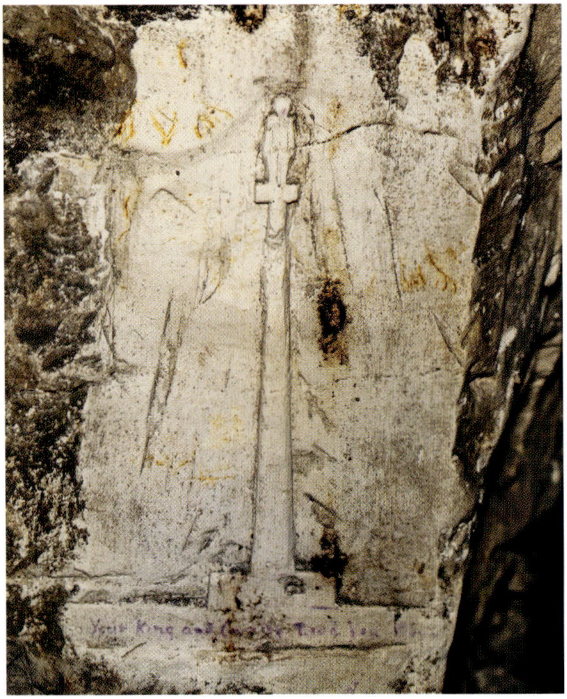

Left: Nelson's Column. The inscription below reads: 'Your King and Country need you'.

Below: The carving echoes Edvard Munch's *The Scream*. On its forehead is written Dr (for Driver) W. F. Holland and A.S.C. (Army Service Corps). It is unclear whether Holland created the work; he may have simply shared its sentiment.

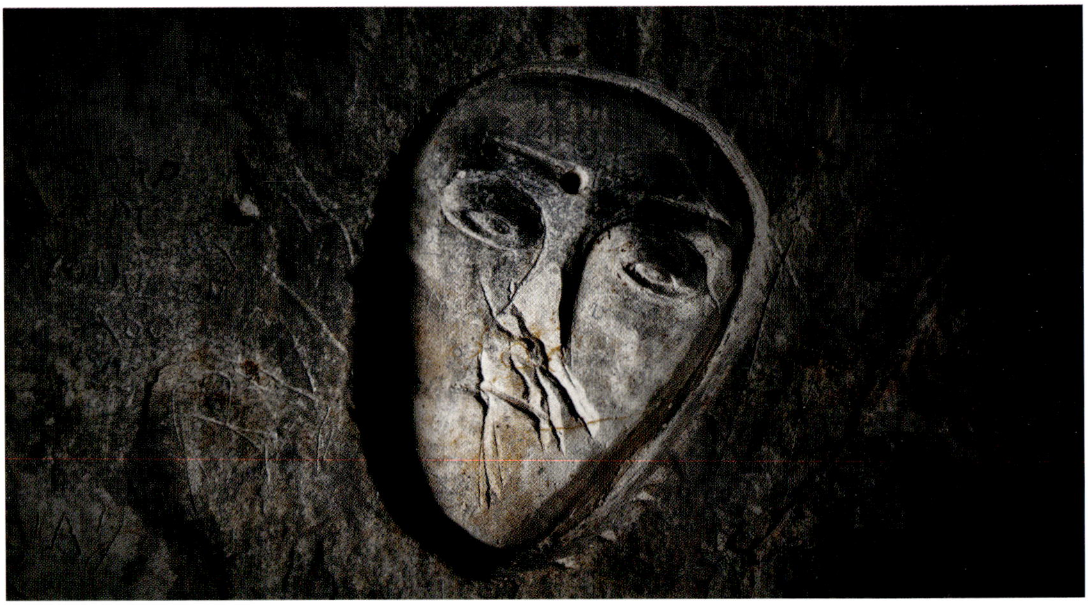

The Durand Group has been working at Maison Blanche since 2006, surveying and recording its artefacts to gain a better understanding of the battle. The entrance to the quarry remains firmly locked under the same three sheets of shrapnel-damaged, German corrugated iron that have protected it for almost a century.

The Banksys of Bouzincourt

The red-brick church of the small farming village of Bouzincourt in the Somme region has a spire shaped like an artillery shell. It stands as a defiant memorial to the obliteration of the village in the First World War.

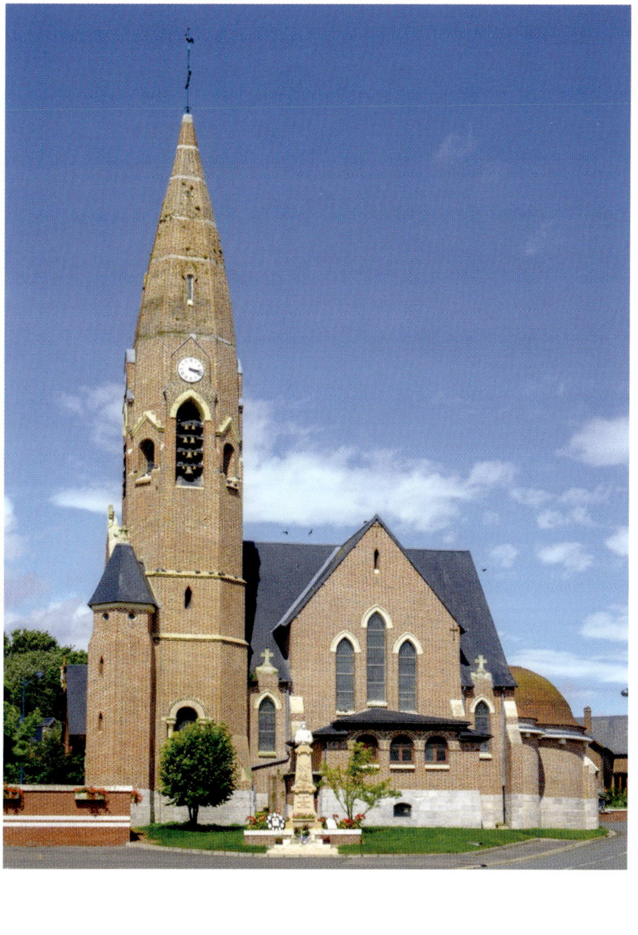

The rebuilt church of Saint-Honoré, Bouzincourt.

Bouzincourt had to be rebuilt from scratch. What lies beneath the church of Saint-Honoré, however, remained intact. It holds a little-known legacy left by veterans of the Battle of the Somme. As you venture into the sixteenth-century tunnel, inscriptions made by British, Canadian and Australian soldiers appear almost everywhere your torch beam falls on. The biggest concentration of names can be found in some of the fifty chambers that lead off the narrow, 120-metre passage. Some were written on the same date by men from the same battalion, standing together at the walls in moments frozen in time on the graffiti-strewn rock. Here too, some of the authors are known to have been killed within days of making their mark, according to the archaeologist Vincent Faivre, who has conducted an exhaustive study of the inscriptions made here.

In a four-year research project, he logged a total of 1,150 traces left by soldiers of the First World War. Most of them date from 1916, but graffiti has also been found from 1917 and 1918.

Faivre's work has brought the history of this hideout to life. He discovered a correlation between the number of inscriptions made per day and the ebb and flow of the Battle of the Somme, and in hundreds of cases he found out who the men were and what happened to them.

The initial inscriptions reflected the build-up to the battle. The first name Faivre found was written in February 1916 by Acting Sergeant Bert Hickson of the Royal Engineers, service number 660, who went on to win the Military Medal for 'bravery in the Field.' Then came the pioneers of the 17th Northumberland Fusiliers, tasked with building and repairing trenches, dugouts and roads. They left fifteen inscriptions between 11 and 17 June 1916.

The volume of graffiti increased as British troops of the 32nd Division piled into the village which was turning into a major military camp in preparation for the big push on 1 July.

At the start of the battle, the village came under intermittent, imprecise but murderous German bombing that claimed a number of lives. The history of the Royal Berkshire Battalion records that on 9 August 1916, 'the cellars of Bouzincourt were full of men, as there was constant long-range shelling going on.'

In those bloody summer and autumn months of 1916 the tunnels were often crowded with soldiers. They warmed the place with braziers, lit it with torches and candles, smoked, drank, played cards and ate their rations. Dozens of empty army issue tins have been found scattered around the site. Boots, rifle ammunition and helmets also remain there to this day, along with a bucket believed to have served as a toilet. 'They quit their war for a short time while they were down there, it was informal,' said Faivre.

And with a bit of time on their hands, they got to work on the soft limestone around them. 'They saw someone had written on the wall so they emulated it, using whatever they had to hand, a pencil, a nail, a knife,' said Faivre. 'It took just two minutes and my name stays forever.' Some 90 per cent of the inscriptions were made by privates and lance-corporals.

Unlike in Naours, the men here weren't on leave – Bouzincourt was just 5 kilometres behind the front line and they had only just been in action or were about to face it. Much of the graffiti left here has a hurried feel. The soldiers didn't have time to get started on anything elaborate, even if they had been so inclined. Their traces reflect the haphazard

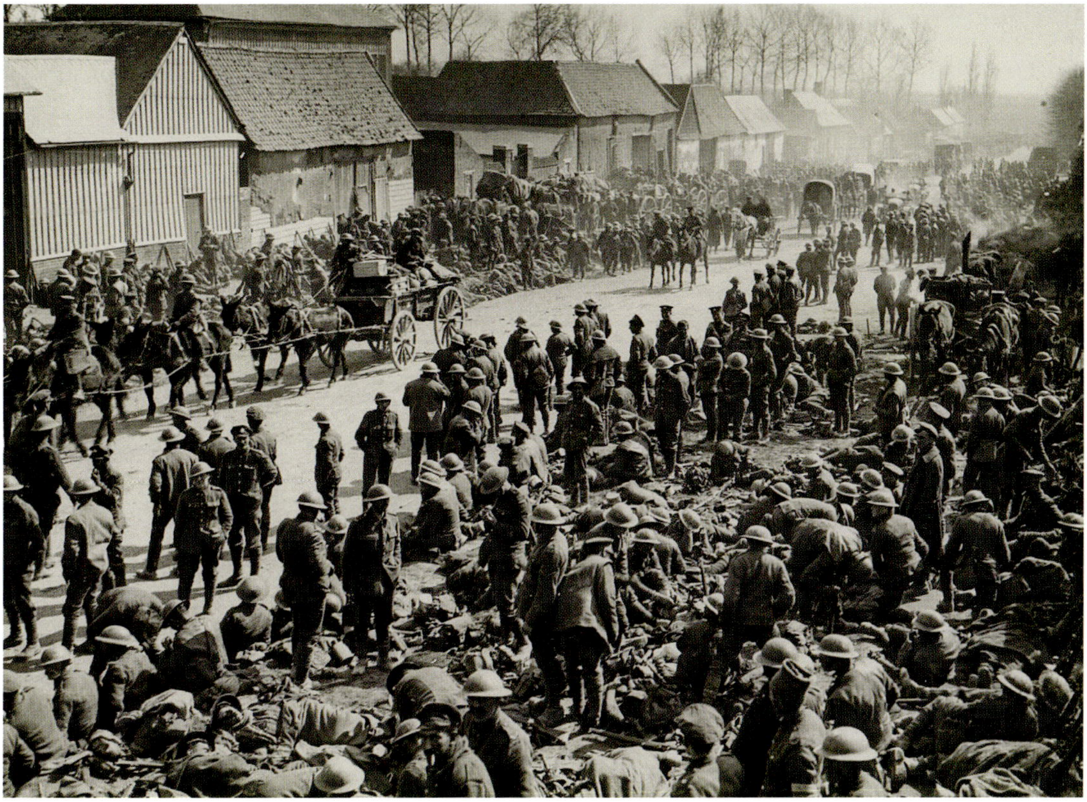

Above: British troops in Bouzincourt. (La Contemporaine VAL 436/138 Producer: British official photo)

Right: Study of a moustachioed dandy crafted by Private Joseph Tagg at Bouzincourt. Born in England, he emigrated to Canada and enlisted at the age of thirty-one. A few days after creating this drawing, he was shot through the right knee, disabling him. He survived the war.

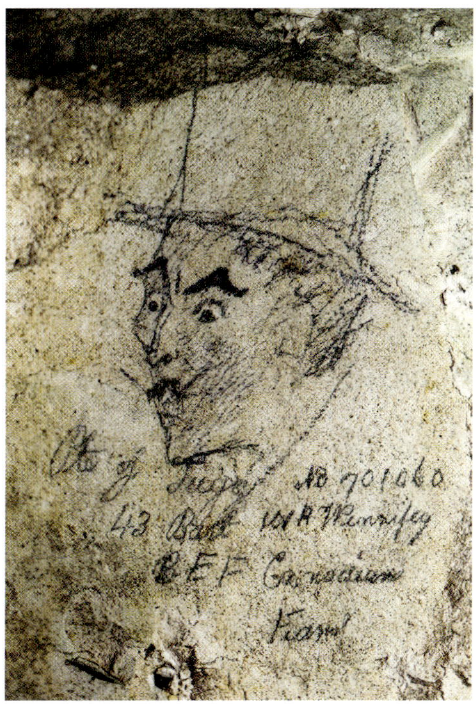

role of the tunnel itself – it remains unclear to this day what purpose was assigned to it during the war because no official records have been found that mention it.

Many inscriptions reflect the pride and confidence of Britain's New Army, made up of volunteers who had flocked to recruitment centres following the outbreak of war. 'DIE HARDS' is written in block letters above the intricately drawn cap badge of the 17th Battalion of the Middlesex Regiment – the famous first Footballers' Battalion, containing professional players, referees, officials and fans from football clubs across Britain. Among them was Walter Tull, one of the first prominent black footballers in league football with Tottenham Hotspur and Northampton Town, who rose to the rank of officer and was killed in action in 1918. Faivre found twenty-one inscriptions by members of the 17th Battalion in Bouzincourt.

One poem signed by 'Pat McCarthy' of A Company of the 2nd HLI (Highland Light Infantry) begins with the line: 'Halt the Greys, Steady the Bays and let the HLI march past.'

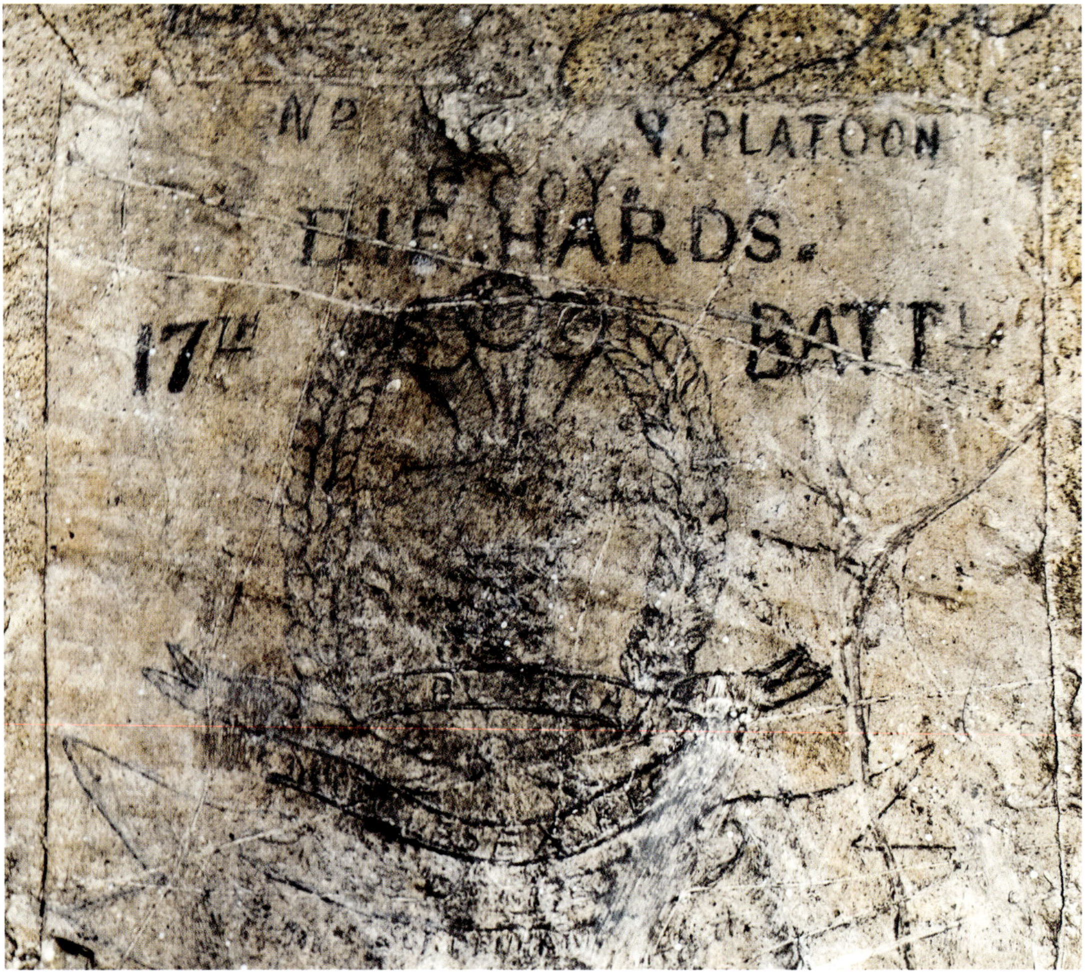

The cap badge of the 'Die Hards' the nickname of the Middlesex Regiment. The 17th Battalion was the so-called first Footballers' Battalion, made up of professional footballers, referees and fans.

Barely legible in faded pencil, it also refers to the 'whitewashed walls of India and the Blood-suckers of Bengal.'

Troops of the Canadian Expeditionary Force began to arrive in Bouzincourt in September 1916 while the offensive was still raging. Faivre found that Canadian soldiers had made 640 inscriptions by the time they left in November and he identified 402 of them with the help of Canada's extensive online archives on its First World War forces.

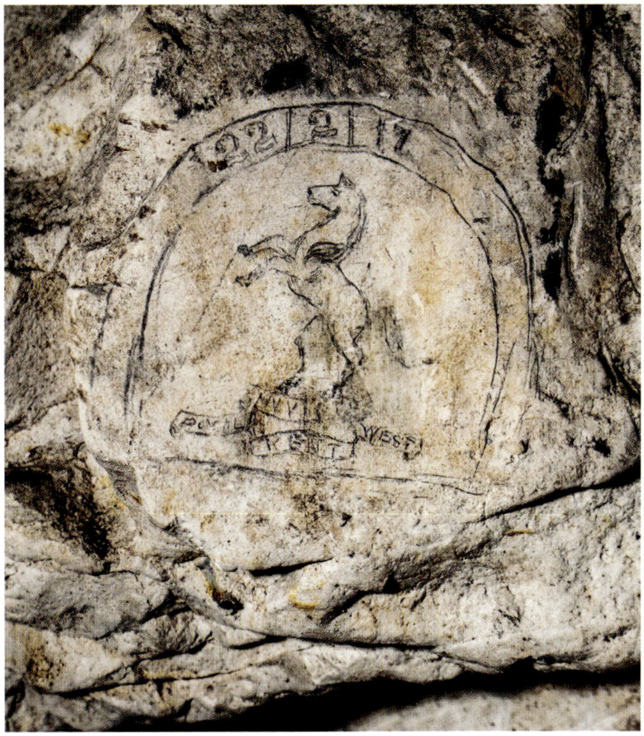

Right: The cap badge of the Queens Own Royal West Kent infantry regiment.

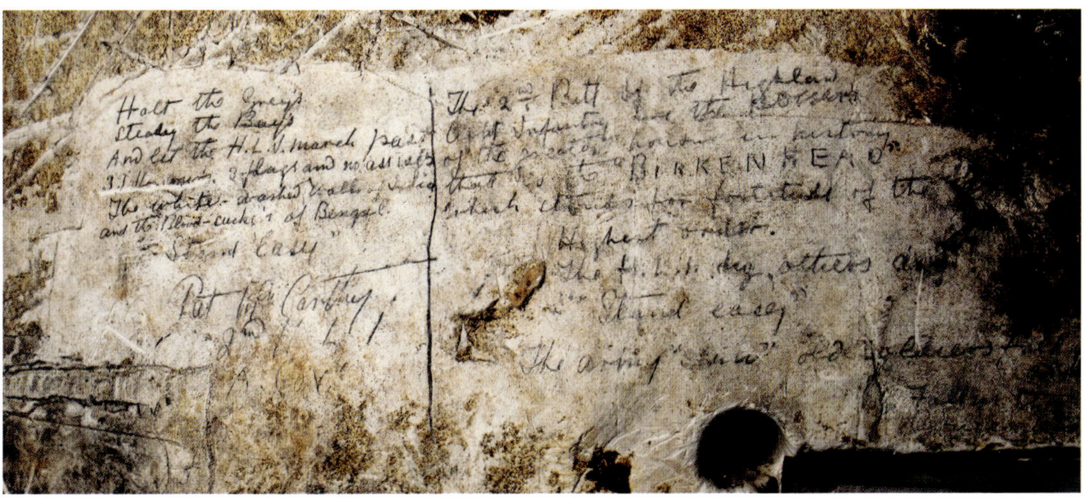

Below: Poem by a proud soldier from the 2nd Battalion of the Highland Light Infantry.

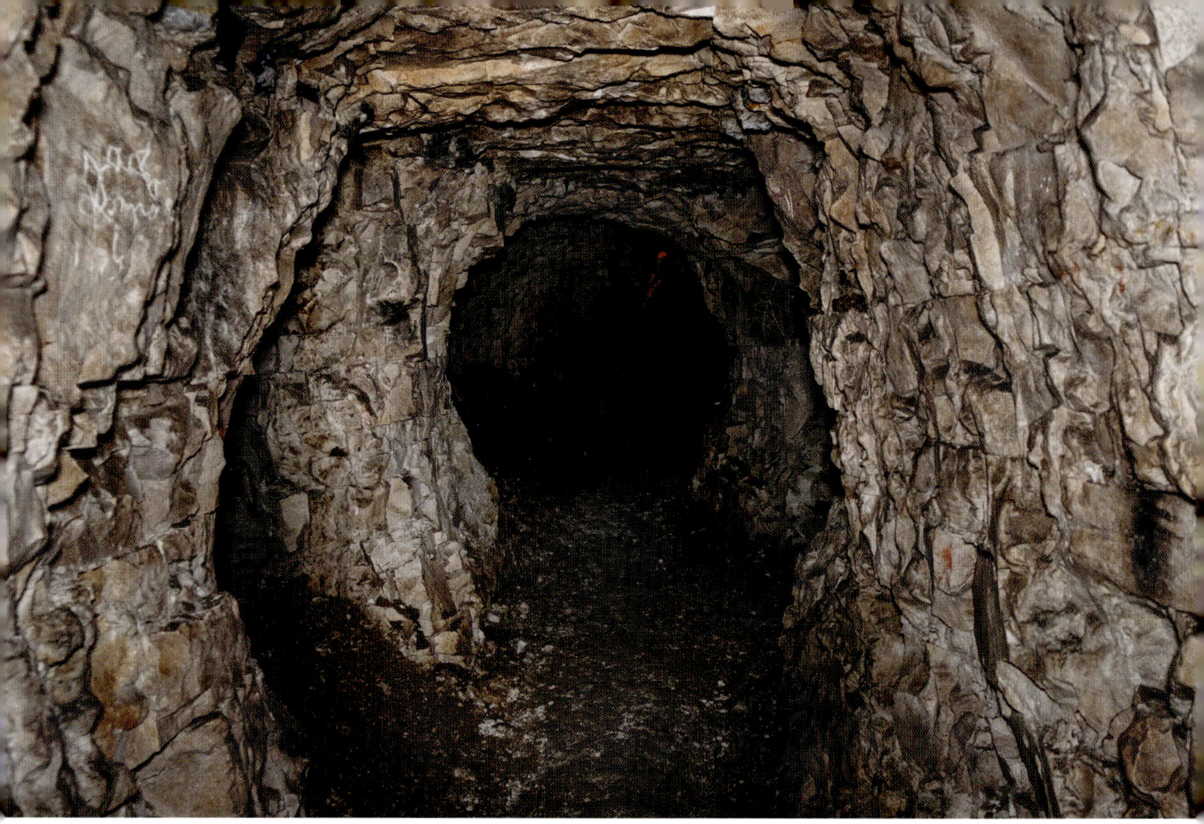

The network is known as the 'Muches de Bouzincourt' in French. 'Se mucher' means 'to hide' in the Picard dialect.

Efforts to identify British troops are more difficult because two thirds of the 6.5 million soldiers' documents from the First World War were destroyed in a fire caused by an incendiary bomb dropped on the War Office Record Store in Arnside Street, London, in September 1940.

Faivre found a total of seventy sets of inscriptions consisting of names written together in a proximity suggesting particular comradeship, with fifty-two containing only two surnames.

But expressions of a wider esprit de corps are far more frequent, with many soldiers naming their battalion, an especially important source of identity due to the make-up of the New Army that went over the top at the Somme. As part of Britain's programme to raise an army of volunteers following the outbreak of war, battalions were formed through local recruitment drives among men of the same city or occupation. Friends, neighbours and colleagues joined so-called 'City Battalions,' known as 'Pals Battalions' in industrial areas of the north of England, attracted by the promise that they would be able to stay together with their mates. But this system of local bands of brothers had disastrous consequences for the communities back home when their units suffered heavy losses. On 1 July 1916, the first day of the 141-day battle, the British Army suffered 57,470 casualties, its worst ever toll, with 19,240 killed and the rest wounded, missing, or taken prisoner, for an advance of only one mile on a part of the front and without breaching the German main second line at any point. More than 5,000 casualties came from London, 5,500 from Manchester with Salford, and over 1,000 each from Edinburgh, Leeds, Bradford and Birmingham. For smaller communities who raised battalions such as the Accrington Pals and the Grimsby Chums, the impact was felt for decades.

The Pals system died that day. The shattered units were replenished with men from different regiments. As one Pal recalled, 'we were two years in the making and 10 minutes in the destroying.'

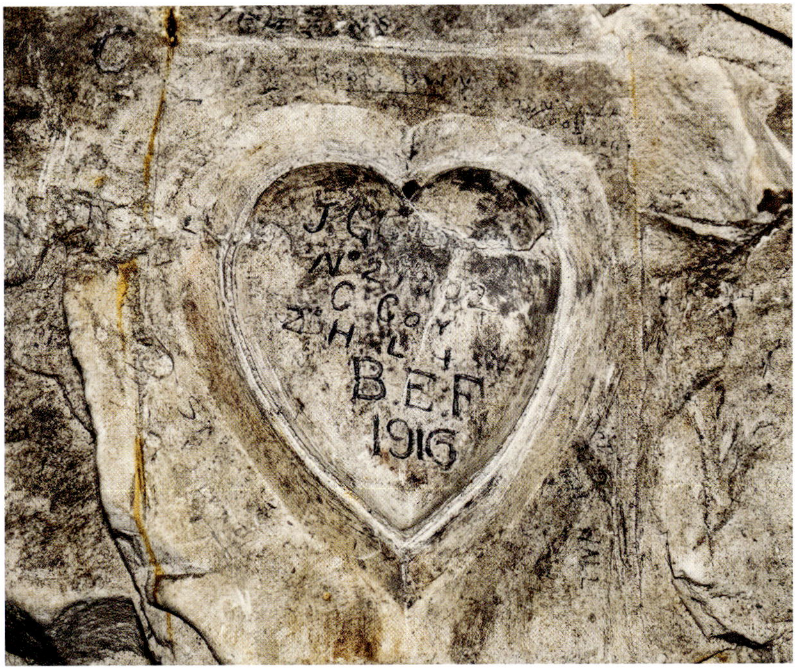

A heart for the British Expeditionary Force.

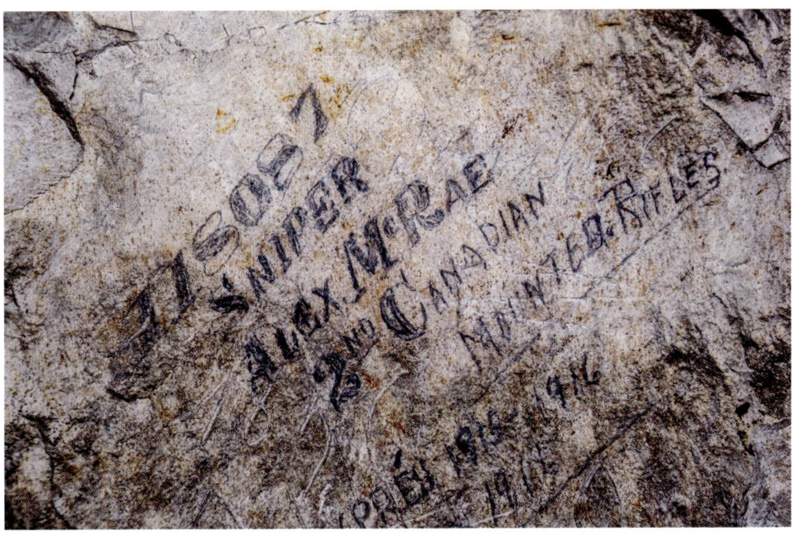

Sniper Alex McRae from Ontario survived the war.

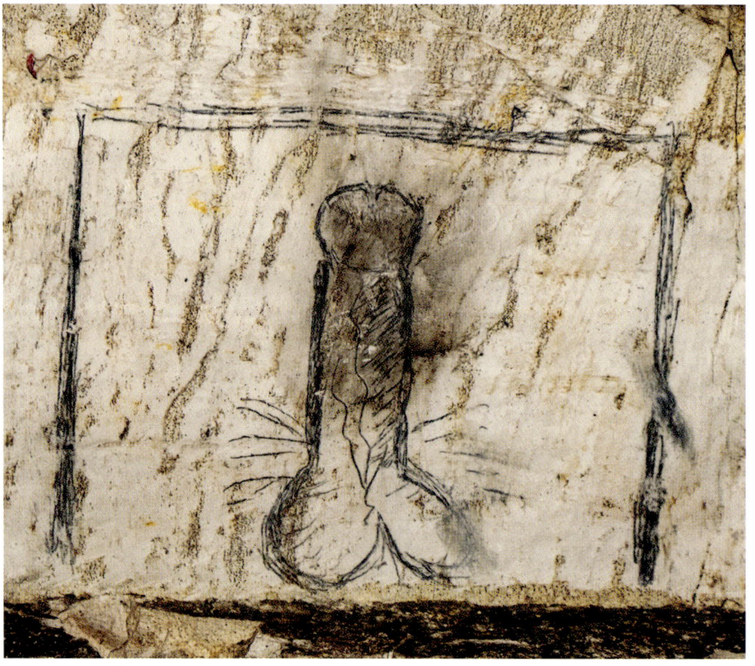

Ageless graffiti, artist unknown.

One carving at Bouzincourt is in the shape of a rectangle to hold a postcard, complete with a groove to allow it to be easily removed with a finger. Inside the space are the number 4612 and the words 'Pte D. McALPINE, 2nd HLI, Wounded 3 times', and 'Glasgow'.

Private Daniel McAlpine, born in 1897, the son of Janet McAlpine of 4 Tureen Street, West Glasgow, enlisted in Glasgow. He was in the Second Battalion of the Highland Light Infantry which according to its war diary spent fourteen days in Bouzincourt in January and February 1917 after fighting in various engagements during the Battle of the Somme. McAlpine's reference to being wounded three times rings with both pride and hope that he had had his share of bad luck and might survive. Five months later, in July 1917, the 2nd Battalion was in trenches on the front line at Cuinchy, some 55 kilometres north of Bouzincourt. It was an ordinary day on the Western Front with no major battle going on – just the routine of repairing trenches, cleaning weapons and watching the front line. The battalion's war diary entry for 16 July was identical to that of the previous two days, stating: 'Companies carried on as usual supplying working parties to front line Companies at night. Our own and enemy T.M's fairly active.' T.M. refers to trench mortar, which could bring death out of the blue. Daniel McAlpine was killed on 16 July. Whether it was a trench mortar, or some other random shell explosion or a German sniper is unclear from the records. Even on 'quiet' days on the Western Front, many hundreds of men were killed. McAlpine was twenty years old. He lies at Woburn Abbey Cemetery in Cuinchy.

Walter Alfred Don Munday, a carpenter by trade but a mountaineer and writer by calling, had not wanted to go war to and later recounted how he took the decision to enlist while standing on a snowy summit in British Columbia. There, he sensed a 'strange coldness' as though the mountains were telling him he was 'unworthy to frequent our shrines' if he refused to make the sacrifice of joining up. He became a scout in the 47th Canadian

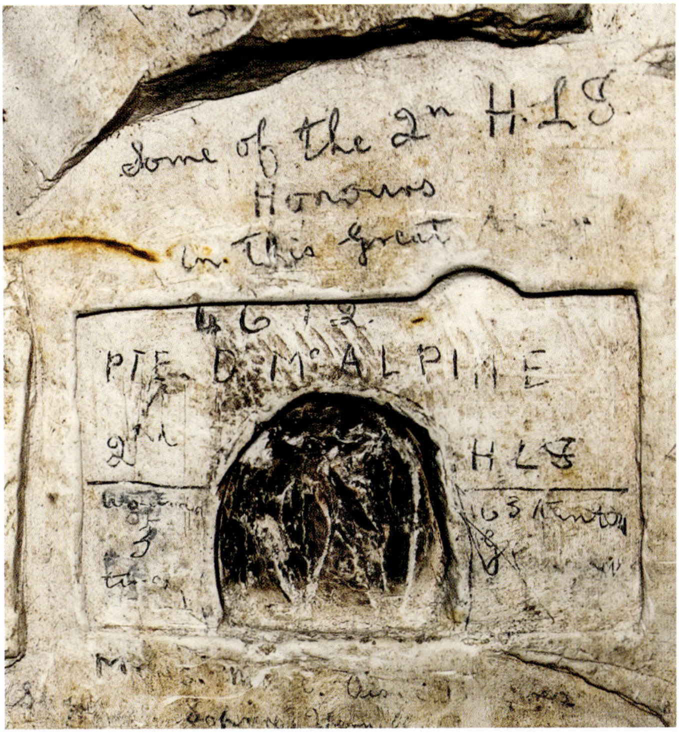

Right: Private Daniel McAlpine, 'wounded 3 times,' of the 2nd Battalion, Highland Light Infantry, did not survive the war.

Below: TMB stands for Trench Mortar Battery.

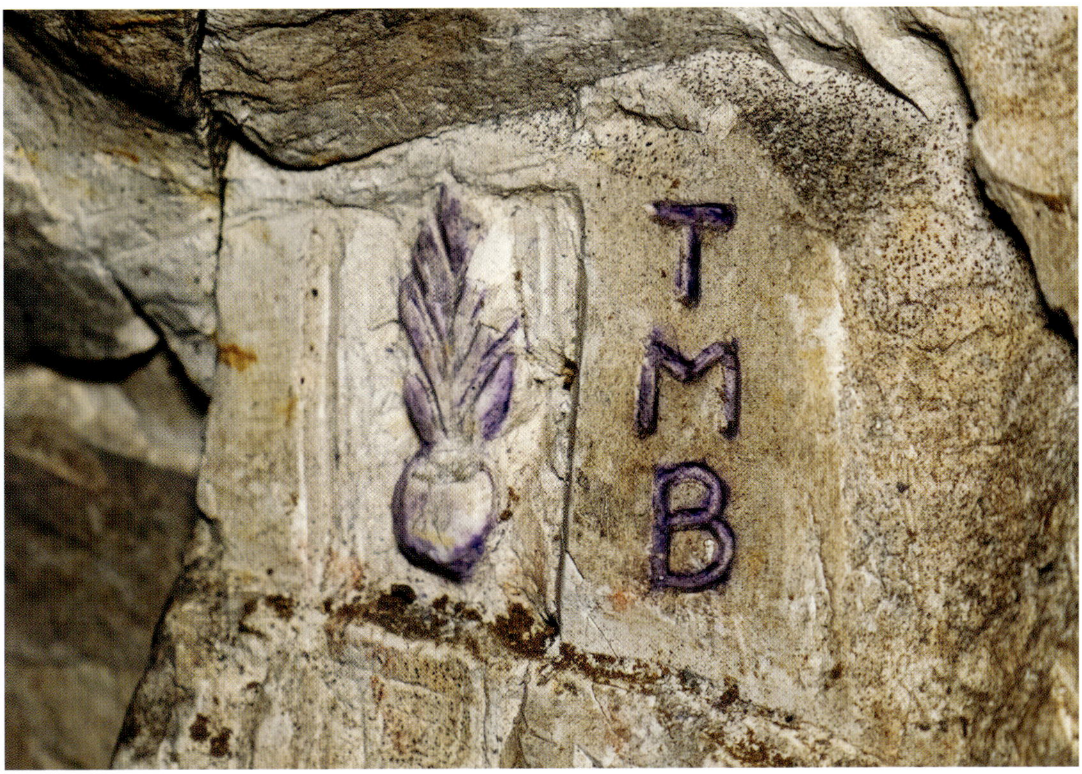

Infantry Battalion because he was familiar with difficult terrain and an expert with a map and compass.

His job was to identify enemy positions and obstacles, usually under cover of darkness, and then to lead troops where they needed to be, and back.

He left his inscription at Bouzincourt on 31 October or 1 November 1916. He went on to win the Military Medal at the Battle of Vimy Ridge, during which he suffered chlorine gas poisoning. On 24 October of that year, at the Battle of Passchendaele, as he was returning from a reconnaissance mission he was wounded by shrapnel, which tore through his left arm from his wrist to his elbow. The wound put him out of the war, and he never fully regained the use of his left hand. He returned to Vancouver and underwent months of physiotherapy and massage to repair the nerves and soft tissue damage. He was discharged from hospital in September 1918. Described as quiet and solitary, he wrote poetry and eked out a living as a freelance journalist and editor. When he first met Phyllis James, who shared his passion for mountaineering and eventually became his wife, she thought he had the look of a lost man. Defying his disability, he returned with her to climb the peaks of British Columbia and the two gained fame as explorers and mountaineers. discovering Mount Waddington, previously dubbed Mystery Mountain, the highest peak in the Coast Mountains of British Columbia. They even have a mountain named after them: Mount Munday, 3,356 metres high, one of the principal summits of the Coast Mountains.

Munday died on 12 June 1950, at the age of sixty-two, of pneumonia – his lungs had never fully recovered from the gassing. Devastated, Phyllis hired a plane and scattered his ashes over the glaciers and snowy peaks he had loved.

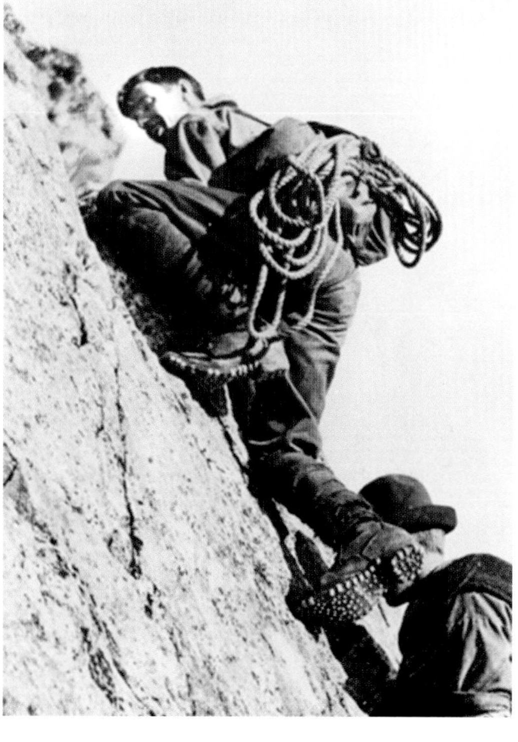

Don Munday climbing in British Columbia after the war. (MONOVA: Archives of North Vancouver, #6316, photographer unknown)

The Suicide Battalion

The 46th Battalion of the Canadian Expeditionary Force was formed in 1915 in the evocatively named city of Moose Jaw in the province of Saskatchewan. It became known as the Suicide Battalion because it was involved in every major battle the Canadians fought in from August 1916 until the Armistice. Of the 5,374 officers and men who passed through the battalion, 4,917 – 91 per cent – were killed or wounded. Thousands of people turned out to give the men a send-off as they marched down Main Street to the railway station. The words to Tipperary were changed to 'It's a long way to Manitoba,' and 'Berlin or bust' was scrawled on one of the carriages as Canada readily answered Britain's call to arms.

Private Roy Klinzing was among the men of the 46th who left their signature at Bouzincourt. He enlisted in the Canadian infantry in Saskatoon on 11 February 1916 at the age of nineteen. He was only 5 feet 4 inches tall, and he could run fast – perfect attributes to become a runner, a key role in a war in which modern communications like the telephone often broke down.

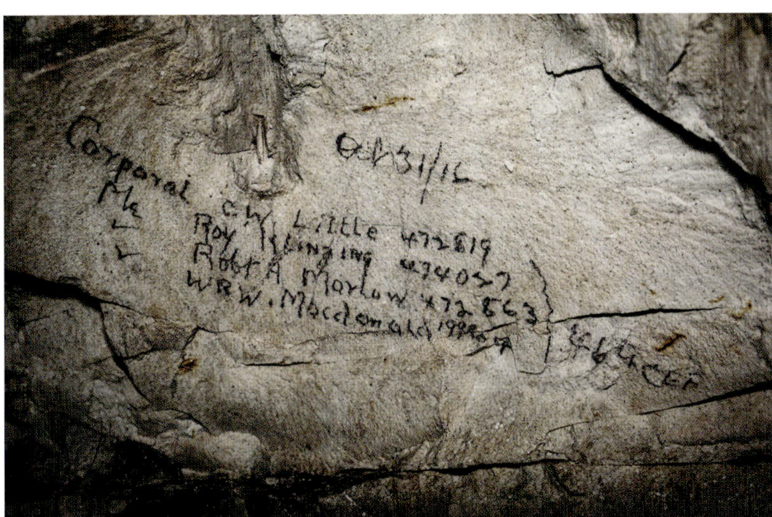

The inscription of Private Roy Klinzing, a runner for the 'Suicide Battalion' who survived.

Before the Battle of the Somme, a huge cable system had been installed but for obvious reasons extended no further than the front line. Once the shooting started, the advancing troops vanished into a fog just when communications were at their most vital. Surface lines, which would be churned up and torn by exploding shells, were in any case easily tapped and morse buzzers vibrating in the chalky ground could be heard hundreds of yards away. Heliographs, which transmitted messages by reflected flashes of sunlight, and flags were also used, but their effectiveness was limited in the smoke of shellfire and at night. The *Wipers Times*, a satirical trench newspaper published by British soldiers, came up with a solution: crossing a parrot with a pigeon. 'It should be of immense use to the War Office as the bird can deliver its message by word of mouth,' it suggested. In the absence of such a 'Parrotidgin,' however, courageous men like Klinzing were needed. The farmer from North Dakota was awarded the Military Medal, the 'Other Ranks' equivalent of the Military Cross (which was only awarded to officers), for an action on 12 April 1917 during the assault on Vimy Ridge. His citation reads:

> Carried on his duties as a Company Runner under rifle and machine gun fire after being buried by a shell and having his arm dislocated. He continued to perform the duties of runner and guide to ration parties for some hours and throughout showed cool indifference to danger.

A few weeks later, on the night of 2/3 June, he won a bar to his medal with another feat of bravery. He survived the war despite being gassed and suffering from shell shock, as post-traumatic stress disorder was called at the time. He died in 1981 at the age of eighty-four.

Alfred Cromwell Myers, a trainee schoolteacher, volunteered to join the Canadian infantry in January 1916. In November of that year, he was sheltering in the Bouzincourt caves and in neat calligraphy that would have impressed his pupils etched his name into the rock wall. That month, he was transferred to the 46th Battalion which had been depleted by heavy losses during the capture of Regina Trench on the Somme, the longest trench built by the Germans on the Western Front. A few weeks later, just before Christmas 1916, the 46th was 50 kilometres north of Bouzincourt, facing Vimy Ridge. The slope was an open graveyard. The French had tried and failed to seize the ridge in 1914 and 1915. The Moroccan Division with their bright red fezzes came closest with a heroic attack in May 1915 but they were beaten back and half a year later many of their dead were still hanging on the German barbed wire, their torn red trousers fluttering in the breeze. In the opening months of 1917, there was continual bombardment by both sides and the men's clothes and equipment were constantly wet. Nevertheless, one veteran called it a 'vast improvement over the Somme.' In preparation for the April attack on Vimy Ridge, commanders ordered frequent trench raids – fifty-five in total – to boost leadership and combat experience, take prisoners, discover the strength of the enemy and locate the entrances to German tunnels driven under no man's land. The men despised the raids because they almost always resulted in Allied casualties. Most raids took place at night. The one Corporal Myers took part in on 19 February 1917 at the village of Givenchy-en-Gohelle was unusual because it started in daylight, at 5.30 p.m. It was intended in part as a message to the Germans: expect us any time, day or night.

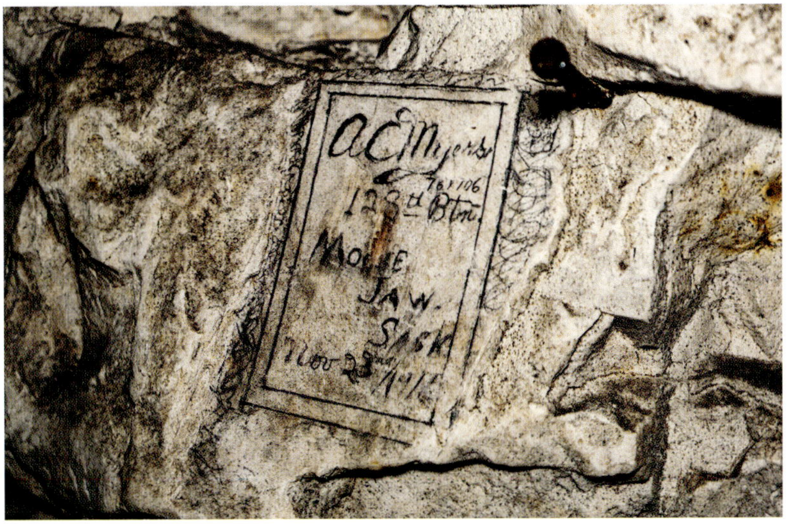

Fine calligraphy: Alfred Cromwell Myers, a schoolteacher by profession.

The official war diary of the 46th Battalion for that day states that the raiding party consisted of ninety-three Other Ranks and three lieutenants.

No prisoners were taken but twelve dugouts, four sniper posts and two machine gun emplacements were destroyed. There were fifteen Canadian casualties, of whom thirteen were listed as having suffered wounds and two, including Myers, were reported missing.

What had happened to him? It is known that he was wounded immediately after he entered a German trench. He sat down in the corner of a traverse and told a comrade he would be all right in a few minutes and would return to his own lines.

When the raid was ending, as Myers' comrades were preparing to leave the trenches, they returned to where he had been sitting and he was gone. German sources later said he had been killed. He was filed as missing and his name was inscribed on the towering Canadian memorial on Vimy Ridge.

Then, in 2015, he was found – at least, probably. Researchers submitted a report to the Canadian Agency of the Commonwealth War Graves Commission concluding that the remains of an unknown Canadian corporal lying in Cabaret Rouge cemetery in Souchez, 5 kilometres from Givenchy-en-Gohelle, had the 'most probable identity' of Corporal Myers. His last minutes may remain a mystery. But his probable final resting place is now known. The well-tended cemetery, named after a French café destroyed by shellfire, has a grand entrance arch and massed headstones laid out in sweeping curves. It overlooks farmland and on a fine day, the Portland stone shines in the sun.

The inscriptions bring the visitor closer to the men who fought, suffered, and died. The relative ease with which many of them can be traced through online archives creates an instant arc between the silent gloom of the souterraines and the present. It was a modern war after all, with gigantic bureaucracies keeping detailed records.

But the closeness is also deceptive. The men's collective readiness to endure the constant threat of death and appalling injury, the loss of their mates, the squalor and stench, the cold and mud, the lice, the back-breaking labour and the drills, for a nebulous cause forgotten within weeks of the first guns blazing places them in a very different age.

Germany's Forgotten Fighters

The soldiers of the Kaiser left remarkably few traces considering that they occupied some quarries for years. Commanders may have declared graffiti 'verboten' as the souterraines were turned into well-equipped military bases with electric lighting and telephone cabling, vestiges of which can still be seen today.

The walls were instead reserved for functional signage such as 'To the Kitchen' or '1st Platoon.'

At the Froidmont quarry near the village of Braye-en-Laonnois, the Germans left only a few dozen personal traces in three years while the Americans who took it over after them created over 1,000 in just six weeks. Froidmont is located metres away from the Chemin des Dames, a 25-kilometre road along the ridge between the rivers Aisne to the south and the Ailette to the north. Fiercely defended by the Germans, that ridge was the front line for three years.

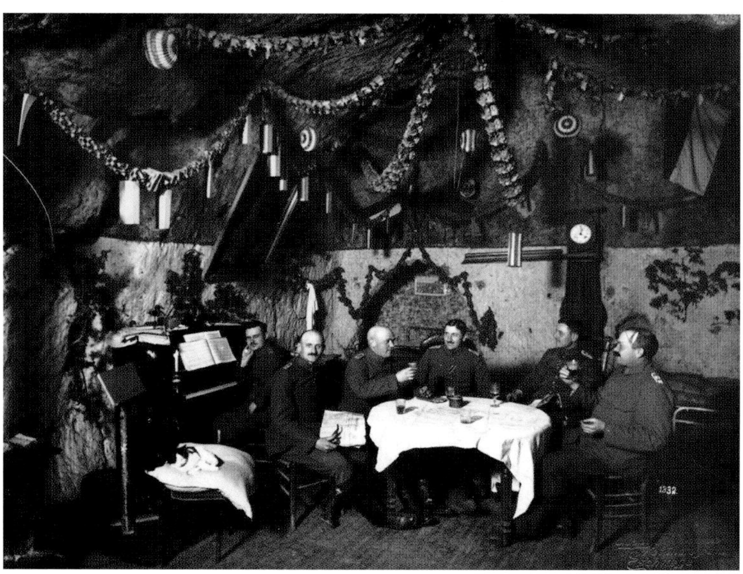

All the creature comforts. German soldiers enjoying a drink in a garland-festooned quarry in Pasly, in the Aisne department, in 1916. Note the piano and grandfather clock, painting and contented cat on a chair – all likely to have been commandeered from evacuated houses nearby (Bundesarchiv German Federal Archive. Photographer: Oscar Tellgmann)

Right: The French amenities were more rudimentary in this souterraine at Leury in the Aisne department. The photo shows artillerymen eating a meal with bottles of pinard. (La Contemporaine VAL 014/162. Producer: Section photographique de l'armée)

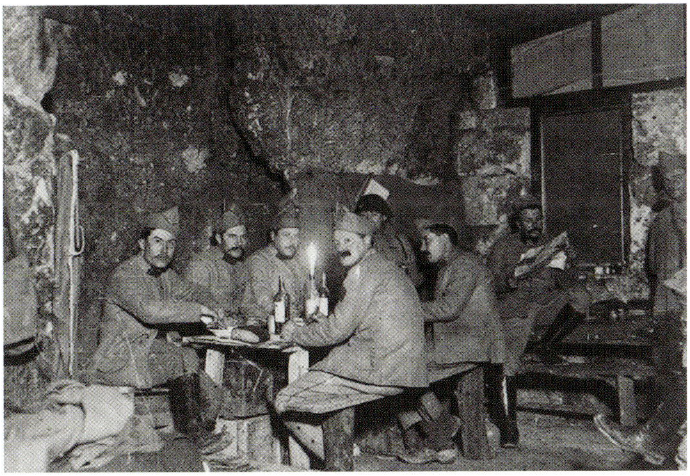

Below: An example of German directional signage – '1st Platoon' to the right.

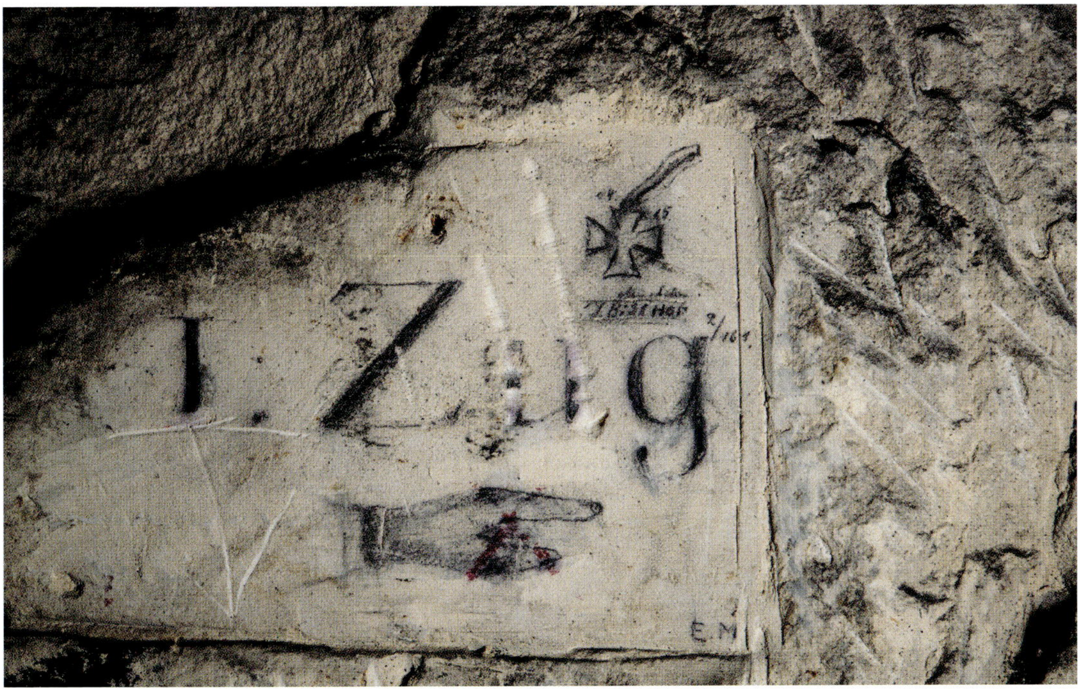

The German graffiti at Froidmont includes imperial Iron Crosses and patriotic declarations such as 'Gott mit uns' which German soldiers had inscribed on their belt buckles.

But some soldiers couldn't resist making their personal mark. One inscription is in memory of Fritz Jaenicke, a Gefreiter or lance-corporal in the 20th Infantry Regiment, the Infanterie-Regiment Graf Tauentzien von Wittenberg. It says: 'Let all the world speak ill of you, just keep your conscience clean, then God will always be with you.' It is dated 14 April 1915.

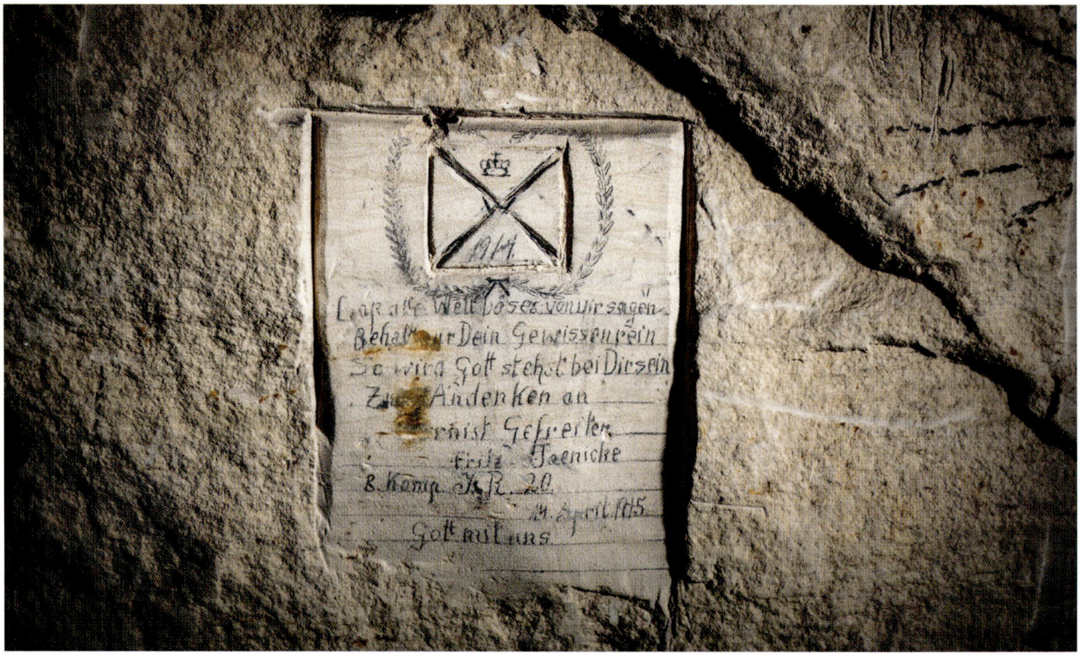

A dedication to the German Gefreiter or Lance Corporal Fritz Jaenicke complete with the ubiquitous slogan 'Gott mit uns'.

One inscription left by soldiers of the 20th Infantry Regiment lists three soldiers inside a carved rectangle underneath a little Iron Cross flanked with two Reich flags. It says: 'Zur Erinnerung an die Kriegszeit 1914–15 Die Krankenträger' ('In memory of the war years 1914–1915 The stretcher-bearers'). The American author Richard Rubin astutely pointed out that the meticulous writing might have been taught by a stern schoolmaster like Kantorek in Erich Maria Remarque's *All Quiet on the Western Front*, the one who led the whole class down to the recruiting office.

It was the same for the Germans as for their enemies, of course. Their mates and their military units became their surrogate families, bonded by their shared experiences.

The historian Thierry Hardier, an authority on First World War graffiti, said the inscriptions left by soldiers on all sides mirrored a conflict within them between their civilian and military identities. While the men readily identified with their military roles and their units, they also wanted to leave a personal, individual trace, said Hardier, who found that of the 4,566 traces he recorded in the Aisne and Oise battle sectors, which includes the Chemin des Dames, 44.9 per cent contained information on the author's identity.

In more than a third of cases, the graffiti also recorded the time it was created, which Hardier said was an attempt to break out of the grinding 'cyclical' perception of time caused by the endless rotation into and out of the trenches, which wrecked their accustomed linear perception of time.

The three stretcher-bearers listed are Friedrich Budschigk, an 'Unteroffizier' ('Subordinate Officer') who was later killed, according to the German casualty list for 2 June 1917. He came from the town of Förstgen near today's German border with Poland. He was twenty-six.

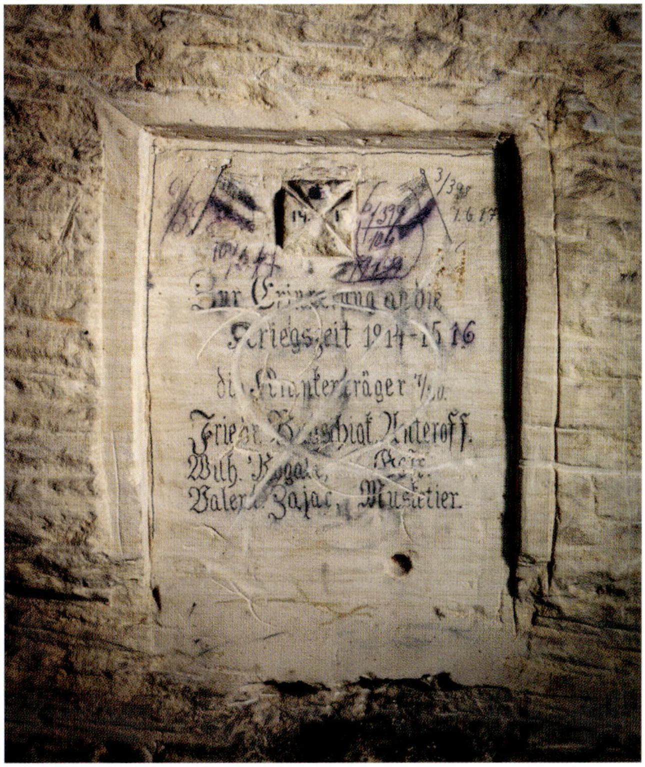

Right: Inscriptions left by stretcher-bearers of the German 20th Infantry Regiment in the Froidmont quarry.

Below: The text on the top right says 'With God for King and Fatherland'.

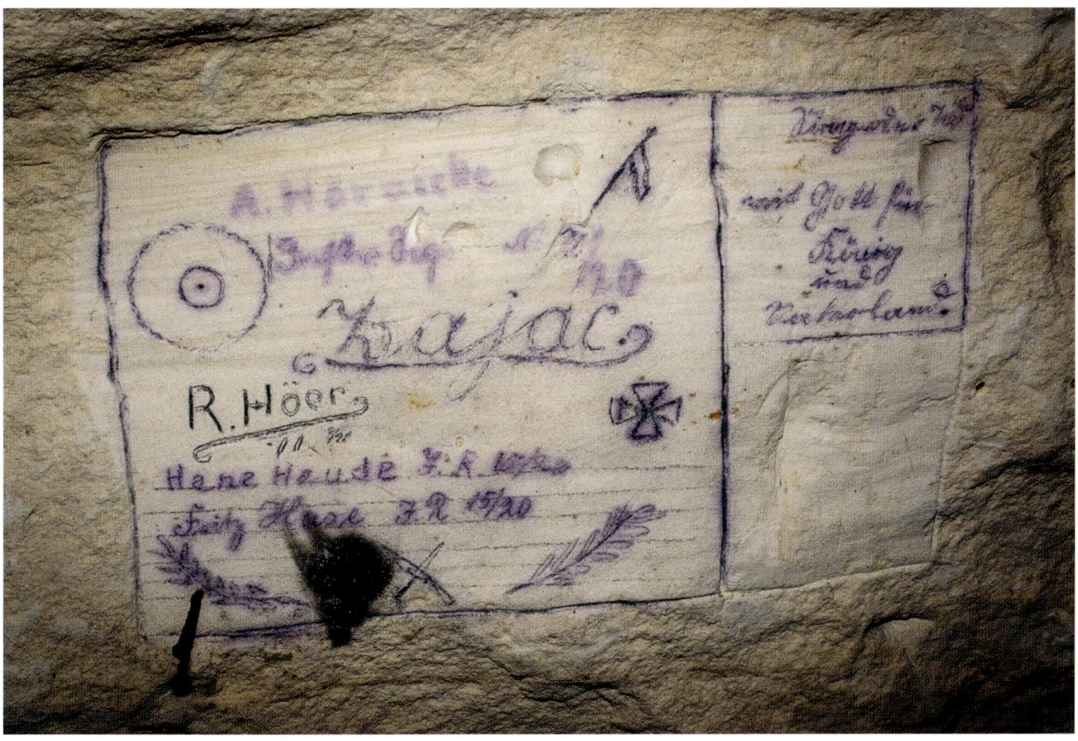

Wilhelm Rogall, a Gefreiter from Beelitz near Berlin, was listed as lightly wounded in the 19 June 1916 casualty list. It is unclear if he survived the war. Valentin Zajac, a Gefreiter from Schmiegel in the Prussian province of Posen in what is now Poland, was officially listed as missing on 6 July 1916.

A little further down the passage, A. Hörnicke wrote his name in purple ink along with six others, including Zajac again, next to the declaration 'With God for King and Fatherland.' The casualty list for February 1915 listed an Alfred Hörnicke of Steinfurth near Berlin as lightly wounded.

Hans Haude, from Berlin, was listed as having suffered a 'fatal accident' in the 3 February 1916 casualty list.

Information about the German authors of Western Front graffiti is comparatively sparse. That is partly because there are far fewer German inscriptions, and they tend to include less personal detail than Anglo-Saxon traces.

Another reason is that there has been virtually no research on the graffiti in Germany, where the 1914–18 conflict has faded from public consciousness. It is generally seen in one disastrous line with the Second World War and lies buried below layers of guilt and shame over the nation's Nazi-era crimes. There is a far stronger historical focus on 1939–45 and unlike in France, Britain, Canada, Australia and the United States, there are no networks of researchers and interested descendants eager to explore individual biographies of First World War combatants.

Added to that, thousands of Prussian army records from the First World War were destroyed in an RAF raid on Potsdam in April 1945. There are other regional archives covering forces from Bavaria, Saxony and Württemberg, as well as city records, and a

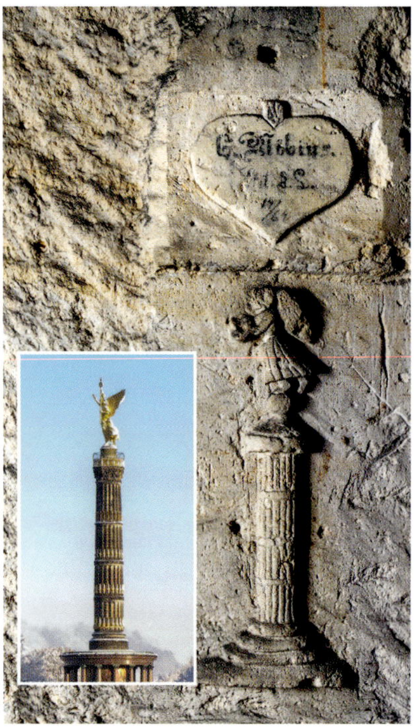

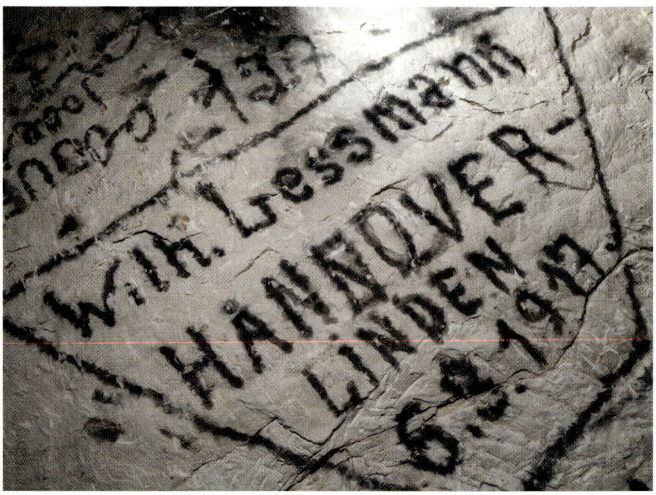

Above: Wilhelm Lessmann of Hanover immortalised himself in soot on the ceiling at Froidmont.

Left: A German sculpture resembling the Siegessäule or Victory Column, a nineteenth-century Berlin landmark commemorating Prussian victories (see inset photo).

recent project has digitised the majority of casualty lists. However, obtaining detailed information on the 13.2 million Germans who served in the Kaiser's armies between 1914 and 1918 remains a hit-and-miss affair.

That said, their graffiti is illuminating in itself. In big letters at Froidmont, one German soldier wrote the latin phrase 'AVE CAESAR. MORITURI TE SALUTANT' (Hail Caesar. We who are about to die salute you'). Seen today, it evokes fatalism, possibly laced with bitter sarcasm. At the time, however, the mindset is likely to have been completely different – a young German soldier portraying himself as a heroic gladiator ready to lay down his life for his emperor. In 1915, when many of the inscriptions were made, morale was still strong.

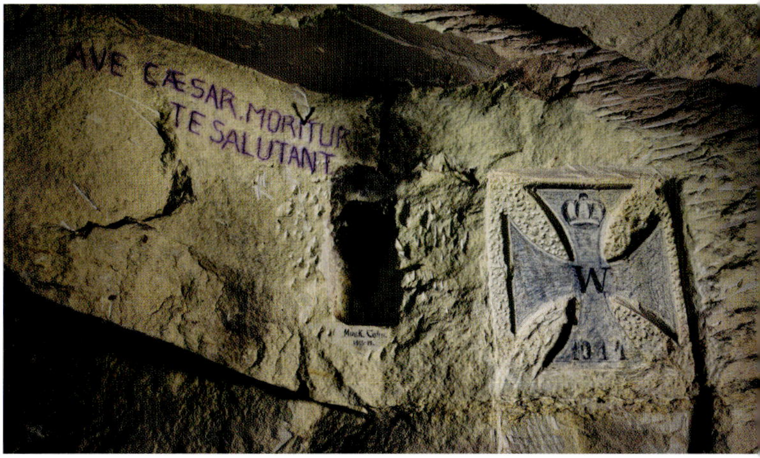

Right: A gladiatorial pledge of sacrifice from a German soldier.

Below: At the Froidmont quarry, German inscriptions in soot.

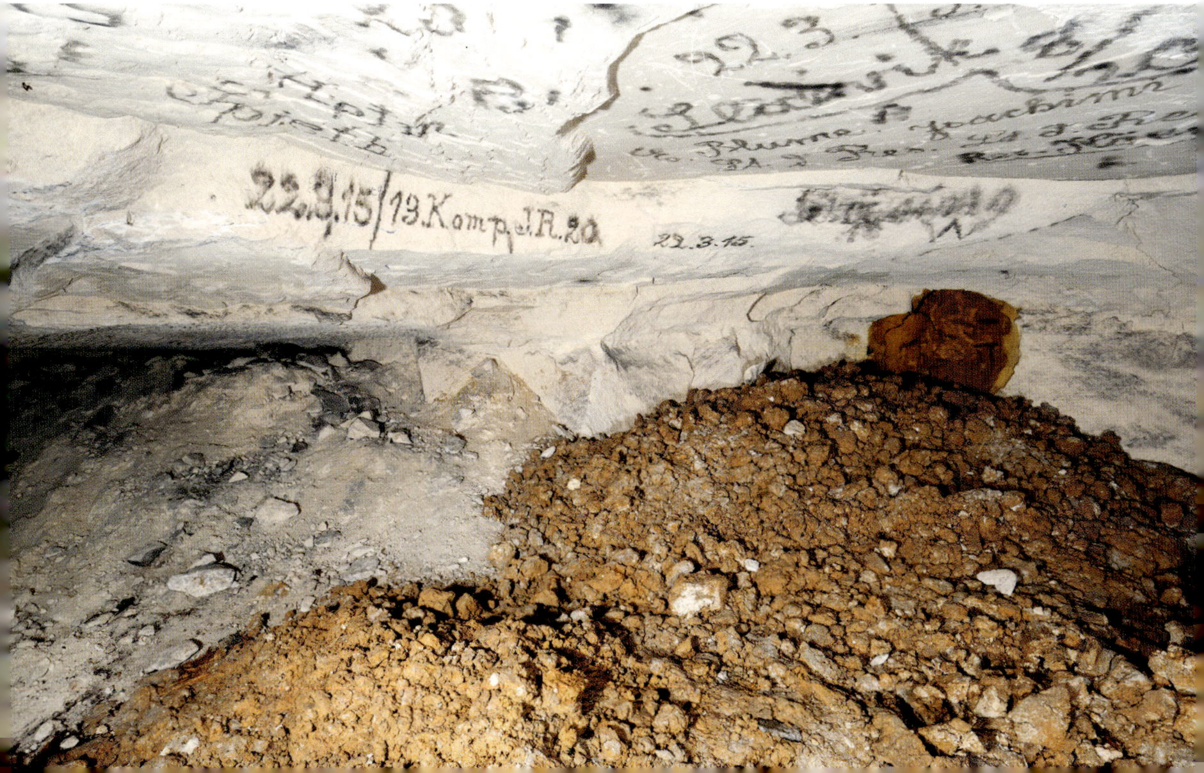

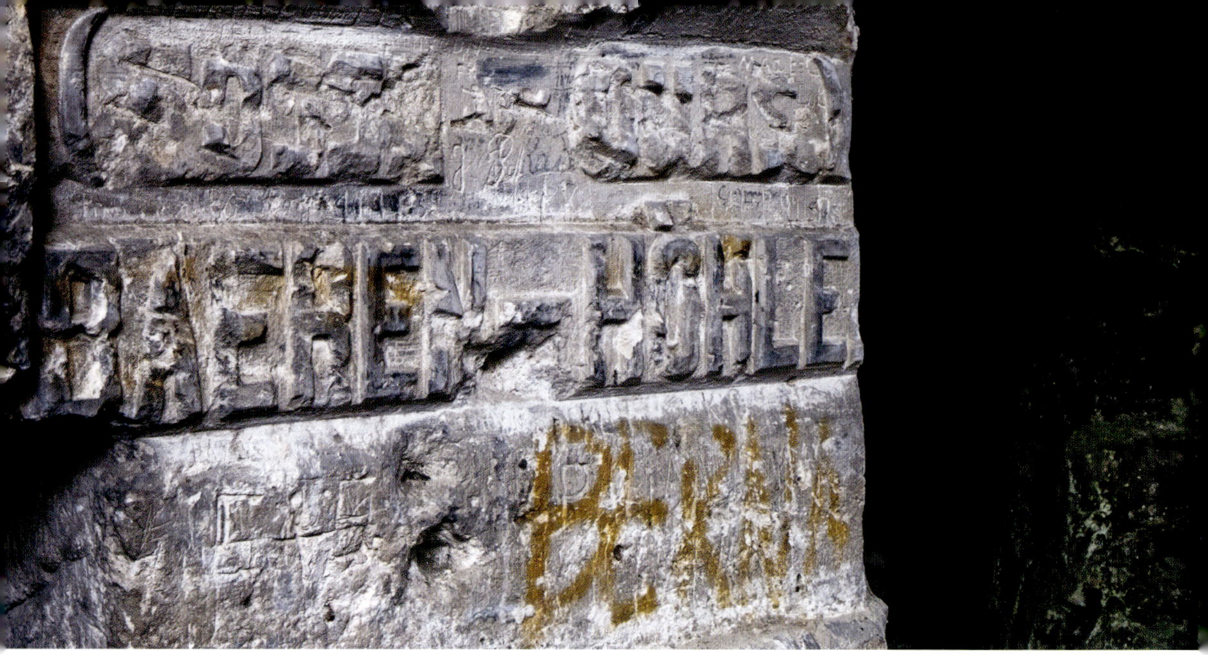

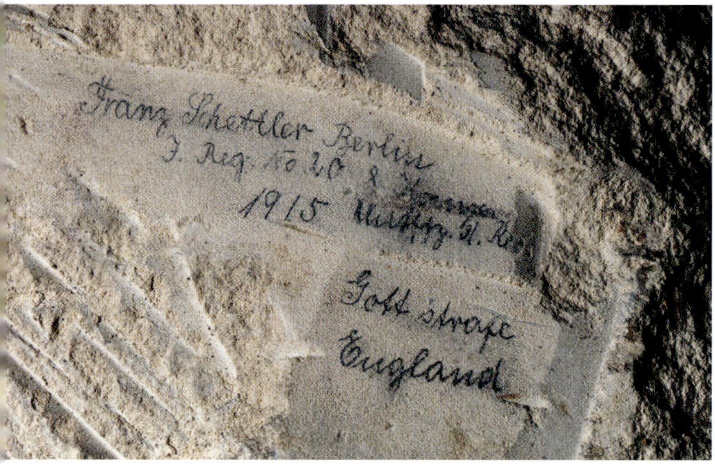

Above: The name 'Baeren–Höhle' (Bear Cave) carved at the entrance to a quarry. The inscription 'Gott Mit Uns' has been defaced.

Left: 'Gott strafe England' was a popular wartime slogan of German propaganda.

Franz Schettler from Berlin wrote the popular anti-British slogan 'Gott strafe England,' ('May God punish England'). This like many other inscriptions, especially German and French ones, reflects the soldiers' bombardment with patriotic emblems and propaganda on wartime postcards and posters, in advertising and on merchandise like bottles, cups and plates.

The German army's underground traces along the Western Front include formidable engineering in the form of brick walls and supports to protect quarry entrances and shore up ceilings.

Some 10 kilometers southwest of Froidmont, in the Rouge-Maison quarry near the town of Vailly-sur-Aisne, some of the Teutonic brickwork is in such pristine condition that it might have been completed yesterday. A century on, it looks set to prevent the tunnels from collapse for a long time to come.

Under Sacred Soil

Deep in the limestone quarry of Confrécourt some 110 kilometres north-east of Paris stands an altar, carved into the wall by soldiers of the French army. It features a bas-relief of a cross surrounded by fiery rays of sunshine under the inscription 'Dieu Protege la France!' ('God Save France!'). It was crafted in 1915 at the request of Paul Doncoeur, the military chaplain of the 28th Brigade. Thousands of soldiers prayed here and sang the Marseillaise before climbing the adjacent steps up to the battlefield above the River Aisne.

Doncoeur risked his life for the men. 'He would go under a veritable rain of steel to pick up in a canvas bag the scattered limbs of the fallen comrades, legs, arms, heads, to give them a decent burial and a last blessing,' Jules Sturn, a sergeant from the 42nd Infantry Regiment, wrote in a letter. The chaplain survived the war and returned to the underground chapel, holding his last Mass there in 1960, one year before his death at the age of eighty.

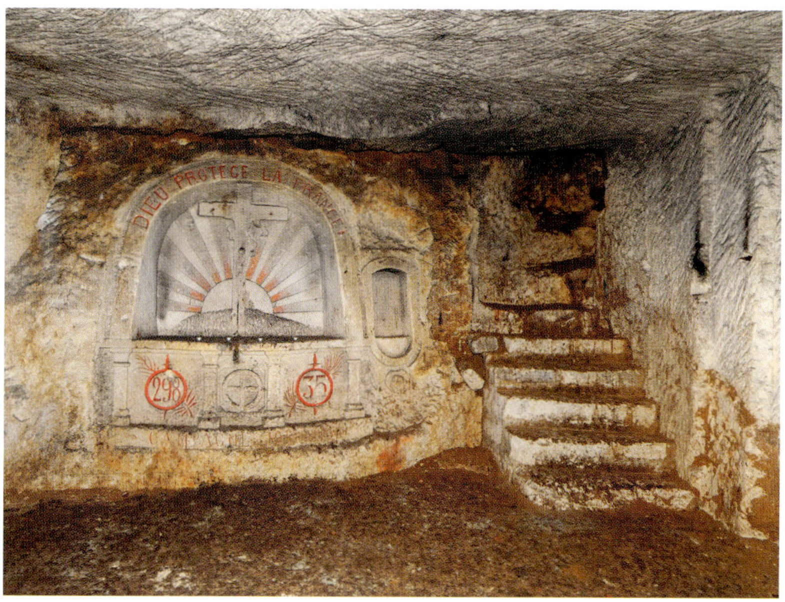

The altar crafted at the request of French military chaplain Paul Doncoeur at Confrécourt.

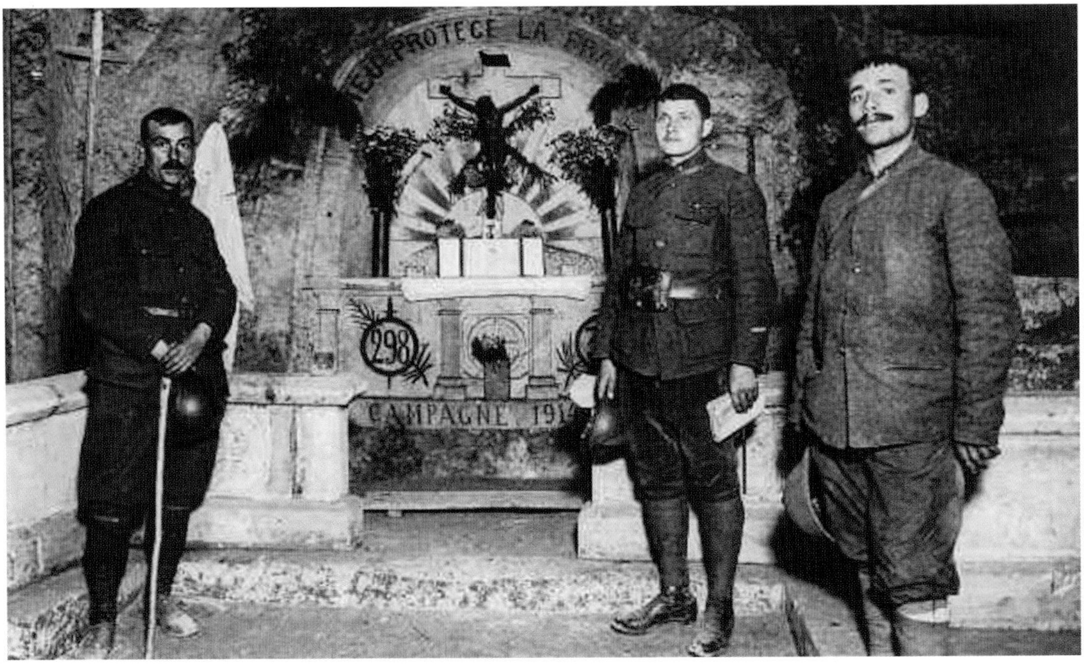

The altar in 1916 with soldiers from the First Regiment of the Zouaves, an elite light infantry formation. (La Contemporaine VAL 012/095. Producer: Section photographique de l'armée)

The front line ran through the fields of the ancient farm of Confrécourt from mid-September 1914 when the Germans, retreating after their advance was checked just 50 kilometres from Paris in the First Battle of the Marne, established themselves on high ground overlooking the Aisne valley. The fighting reached Confrécourt before the beet fields could be harvested. At night, in the moonlight, the plants were a haunting sight as they swayed in the wind. The writer Émile Clermont, who was a sergeant in the 238th Infantry Regiment, recalled: 'In the middle of the beet fields it was easy to imagine in the darkness that troops were crawling along the ground because of the perpetual motion of the leaves.' The exhausted soldiers, fearing surprise attacks, would fire at the swaying plants.

It was here, in the First Battle of the Aisne in September 1914, that the conflict turned into a war of trenches as both sides, facing unsustainable losses from artillery fire and machine guns, dug into the ground.

For the soldiers on the Confrécourt plateau, the limestone quarries underneath them were an unexpected godsend. The temperature was an unchanging 10 degrees all year round, and the troops quickly transformed the subterranean spaces into barracks, installing telephone lines, kitchens and chapels. In early 1915, one soldier described the atmosphere under the fields of Confrécourt:

> Like Roman catacombs, galleries open up. The main alley branches off into regular corridors that go down to the deep chambers, here on our right is the officers' quarters, on the left the quartermaster's room. The non-commissioned officers can warm

themselves voluptuously in front of a large fireplace ... A dry shelter, straw, some furniture, fire, it is a great luxury for the men who come down from the trenches.

The 'Poilus' (literally the 'hairy ones,' the nickname for French soldiers during the First World War) could rest on straw laid out in the candlelit tunnels, smoking, eating, playing cards, writing letters or sleeping.

The engravings they made include depictions of loved ones, names of the fallen, elaborate regimental tableaux commissioned by commanders and, spectacularly, a bas-relief of Marianne, the French national symbol, inspired by her profile on a French coin. While many of the authors, or rather artists, genuinely embraced the exhortation to patriotic duty and sacrifice in the propaganda all around them, there was also an element of convenience in their borrowing of national slogans and images. Many were simply trying to adorn their surroundings and escape their world for a few hours in a flourish of concentrated creativity. The walls made a perfect canvas.

'By trying to create something of beauty, the soldiers were seeking to reintroduce the 'human' into a war that was profoundly dehumanising and had robbed them of their individual identity and locked them in military collectives,' said the historian Thierry Hardier.

The graffiti reflects the patriotism and religion that helped many soldiers get through their ordeal. Hardier found that 8.1 per cent of the 4,566 traces he recorded espoused the men's attachment to their nation and 6 per cent to their faith. Religious symbols, including entire chapels carved into the walls, are especially evident in traces left by the predominantly Catholic French, but also by Catholic immigrants among the US troops.

However, graffiti displaying affiliation with the men's military units was far more common, amounting to 17.4 per cent of the total inscriptions recorded by Hardier. Perhaps most surprisingly, expressions of hatred for the enemy were found in only 0.15 per cent

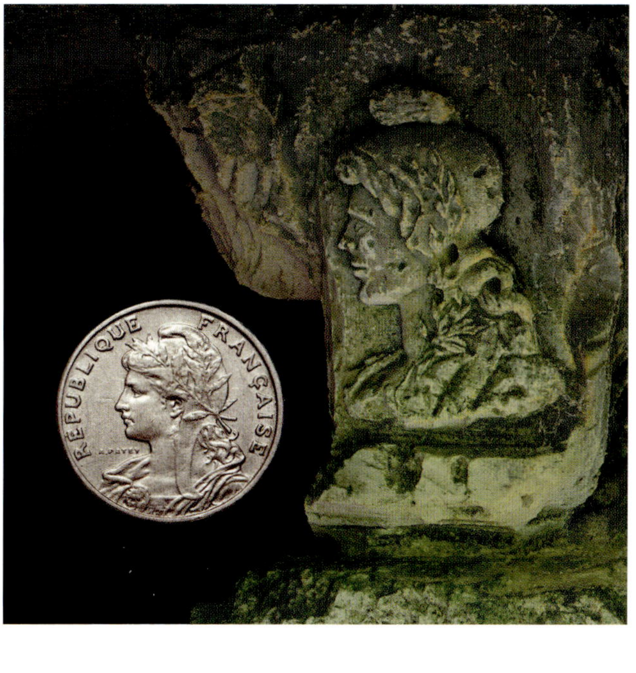

A bas-relief of Marianne, the French national symbol, alongside the 25 centime coin that is believed to have served as the sculptor's model.

of cases. This chimes with recent research showing that informal truces at Christmas and other times of the year were far more frequent than previously thought. 'While many soldiers were of course brutalised, I think people shouldn't equate the willingness to fight with brutalisation or hatred of the enemy,' said the German historian Thomas Weber.

The men also carved everyday objects such as bottles of pinard, the cheap red wine they treasured. Victor Brindeau of the 262nd Infantry Regiment inscribed his name between two small columns decorated with roses and shells. On top, he drew three objects dear to the Poilu's heart: the mug for the 'jus' or coffee, the canteen for 'pinard' and the bowl for 'rata,' a coarse meat stew. Brindeau's war record states that he was 1.63 metres tall, had clear blue eyes, and was born on 19 September 1894 in the village of Gesvres in north-western France. His profession was a road mender. He served for most of the war, receiving citations for courage and intelligence, and survived.

While Brindeau left his name, many of his French compatriots did not bother to sign their works. One explanation may be that they, unlike their Anglo-Saxon comrades, were fighting on their home soil.

The fortress-like ancient farm of Confrécourt, built by Benedictine monks in the ninth century, became a French Rorke's Drift on 20 September 1914, when the German First Army of General Alexander von Kluck attacked it as part of an offensive to drive the French back south across the Aisne. As its ancient walls crumbled under German shellfire, 400 French soldiers withstood attacks from 6,000 German troops. 'The enemies managed to advance up to about fifteen metres, but very few went further,' wrote Émile Clermont.

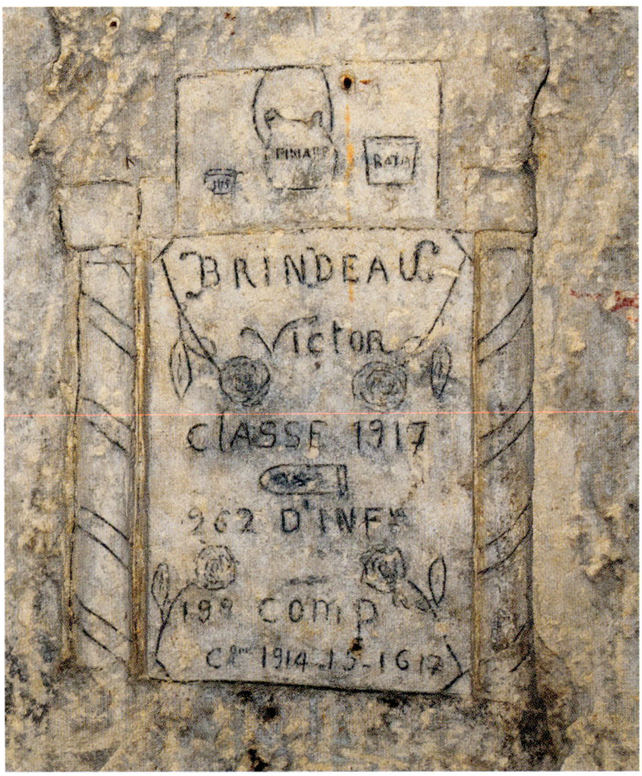

Victor Brindeau's ode to coffee, pinard and rata.

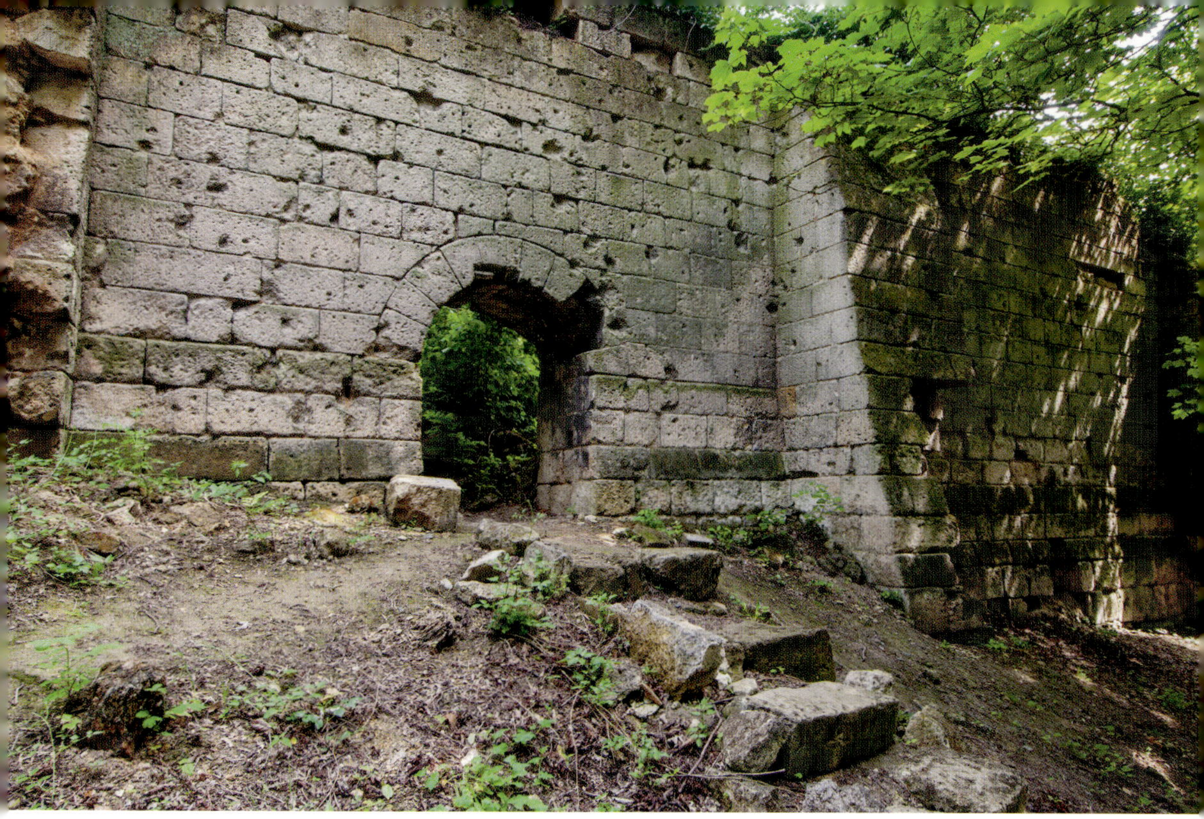

Battle damage on the ancient Benedictine farm of Confrécourt.

'The defenders were determined to do their utmost to hold on. The fight lasted 3 hours. The corpses piled up around the farm.' Finally, Colonel Robert Nivelle, an artillery officer who would eventually become commander-in-chief of the French armies on the Western Front, launched a devastating barrage with rapid-firing 75mm field guns which together with a flanking attack by French 'chasseurs,' or light infantry, rushed in from the village of Vingré repelled the Germans.

Jean-Luc Pamart, who farmed the fields of Confrécourt, used to play hide and seek in the quarries when he was a boy. He remembers old Poilus visiting the former battlefield. The last one came in 1980. He looked lost as he wandered around the plateau and kept asking where 'Hill 150' was. He was referring to a ridge the Germans occupied from September 1914 to March 1917. Pamart has campaigned successfully to preserve the artistic legacy of the troops who sheltered under his soil. Like farmers up and down the Western Front, he has braved the hazards of the 'iron harvest' of munitions that are ploughed up year after year and still claim lives. A large proportion of shells fired during the war – estimates range from one in six to one in three – failed to explode and remain live. Grenades, when caked in earth, can bear a lethal resemblance to potatoes and have been discovered in sorting machines. An added danger comes from sudden collapses in fields as tunnels below them cave in after rainfall or under the weight of combine harvesters. A classmate of Pamart's died aged twelve while trying to dismantle a shell he had found. A neighbouring farmer was killed when a shell exploded in a fire he had lit to cook his lunch by the side of a field.

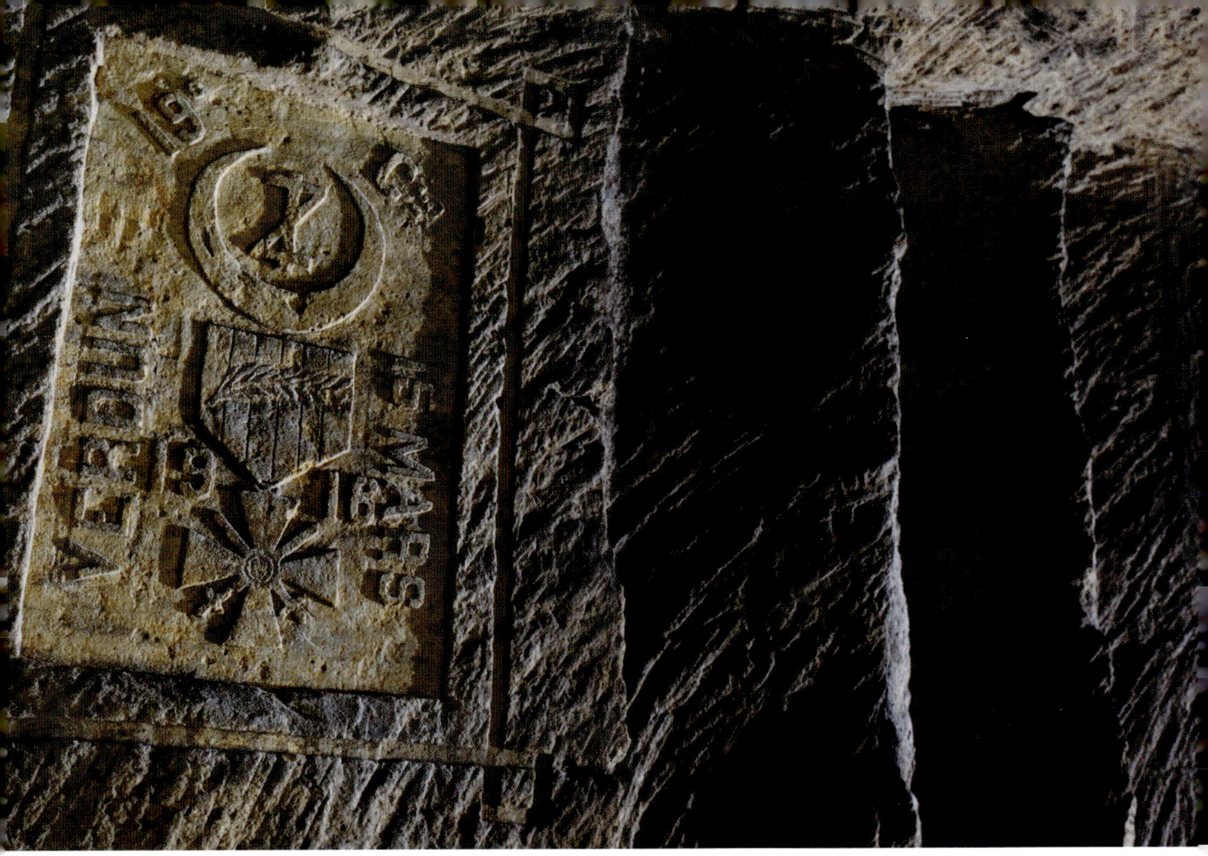

Above: A carving in Confrécourt in honour of the Croix de Guerre decoration won by the 19th Company of the First Regiment of Zouaves at Verdun for an action on 15 March 1916.

Below: Regimental panels carved at Confrécourt in a souterraine known as the 'Carrière du ler Zouaves' in honour of one of the regiments that occupied the quarry.

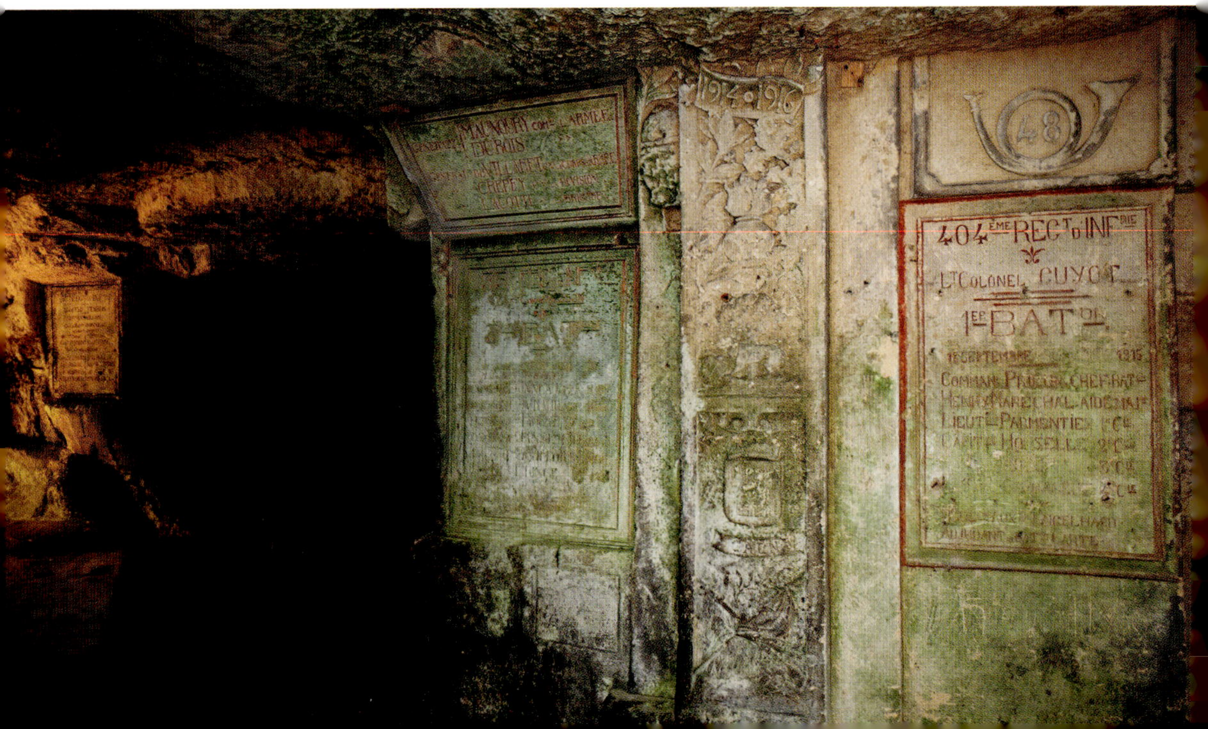

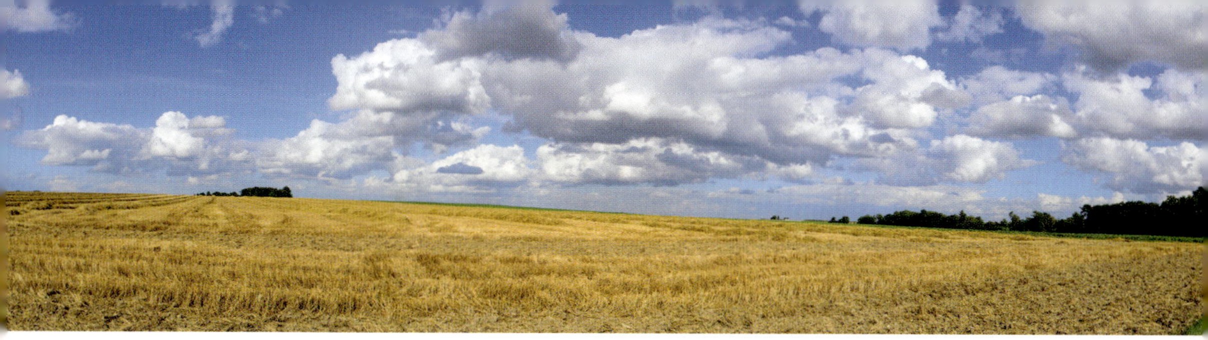

Sacred soil: the fertile Confrécourt plateau, a former battlefield where munitions are still found. The German trenches ran across the horizon.

After the war, the fields that had for centuries delivered an abundance of crops were a moonscape of shell craters and barbed wire. Skeletal tree stumps bristled with shrapnel. German prisoners of war were brought in to help with munitions clearance – a lethal job, as the many German headstones from 1919 in the area show. The first fields were planted again in 1921 but it wasn't until 1932 that the full 250 hectares of Confrécourt were back in cultivation. The farmers were surprised to see the wheat growing so vigorously in some places that the stalks bent under the weight of the ears. Beneath those fertile pockets, the bodies of soldiers were often found.

Pamart believes the inscriptions in Confrécourt and along the Western Front exert a powerful magnetism to this day. 'Isn't sculpture in the hell of war a profound sign of humanity?' he wrote in his book *Le Paysan des Poilus* ('The Farmer of the Poilus'). That humanity was lacking in commanders, as a notorious abuse of human rights showed in November 1914. A few hundred metres from Confrécourt, near the village of Vingré, six soldiers of the 298th Infantry Regiment were chosen by lot and executed after officers decided that their unit hadn't shown enough vigour in a clash with German forces.

Around 60 per cent of the estimated 9 to 11 million military deaths in the First World War were per cent by artillery. The shells blew men to pieces, even atomised them, leaving no identifiable trace. Only half the British Army fatalities of the war are buried as known

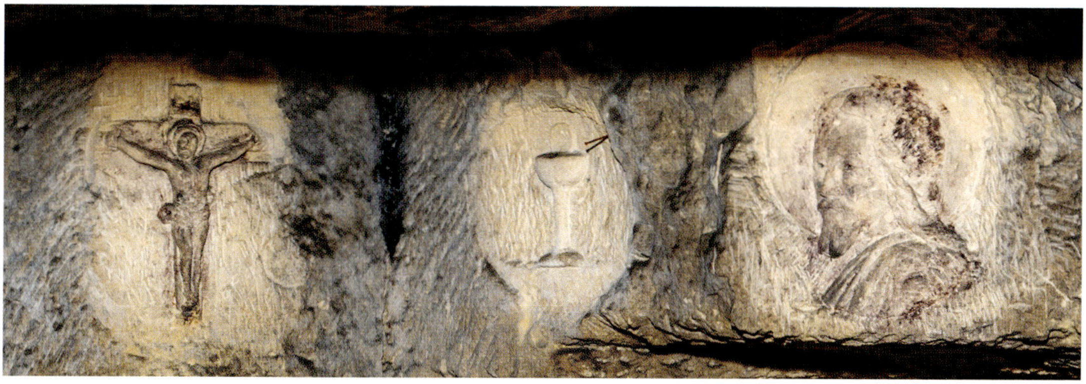

A portrait of Christ in a chapel hewn into the rock by French soldiers in a quarry near the Chemin des Dames.

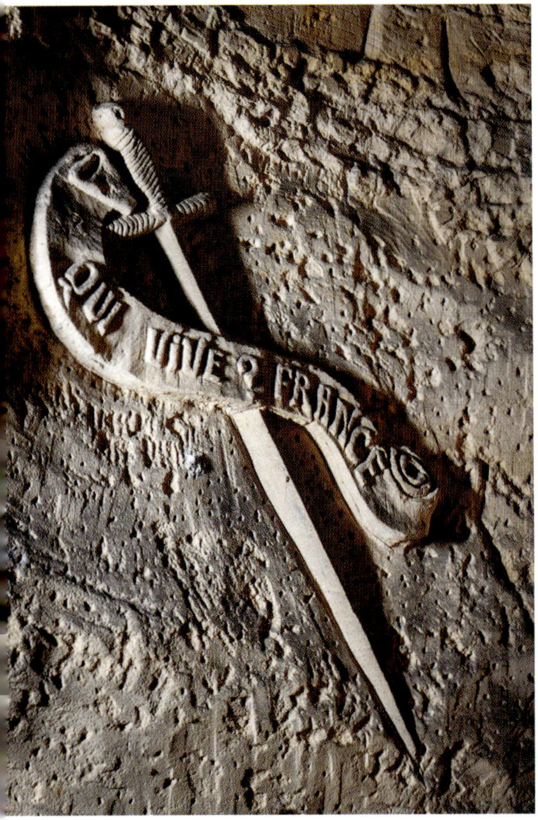

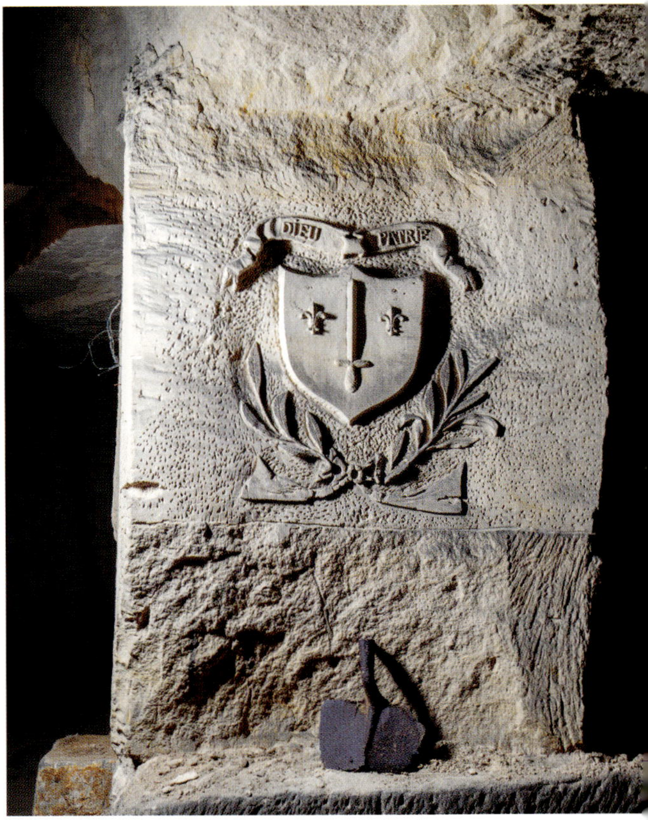

Above left: A French carving in a quarry near the Chemin des Dames bearing the patriotic motto 'Qui Vive? France'.

Above right: 'God and Country' – a French carving in a Chemin des Dames quarry.

Below: What they were fighting for: a French bas-relief representing the most famous monuments of Paris. From left to right: Sacrè-Coeur, the Arc de Triomphe, the Eiffel Tower, the Opera and Notre Dame Cathedral.

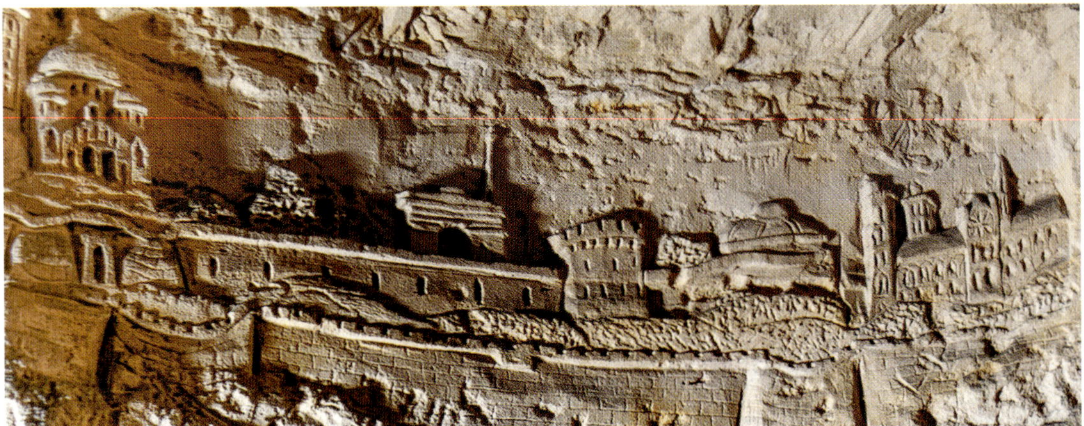

soldiers, with the rest – over 520,000 – either buried but unidentifiable, or unburied. The inscriptions 'Known unto God,' 'Soldat Inconnu' and 'Unbekannter Soldat' are ubiquitous on headstones in the hundreds of cemeteries along the Western Front.

During the war, the French High Command responded to the surging death toll by ordering the burial of soldiers in mass graves of up to 100 bodies. But the men refused to accept the anonymity of their comrades. 'Sergeant Guitard killed at this spot on 27 January 1916,' says one unsigned inscription decorated with an olive branch. One panel is dedicated to the dead of the 35th Infantry Regiment, listing them chronologically as the fighting claimed them.

The murals of Confrécourt testify to the Poilus' battle not to be forgotten. A century on, the heritage society Soissonnais 14–18 set up by Pamart is waging it on their behalf. He believes he has a duty to keep alive the memory of the soldiers who fought and died for the land he tilled.

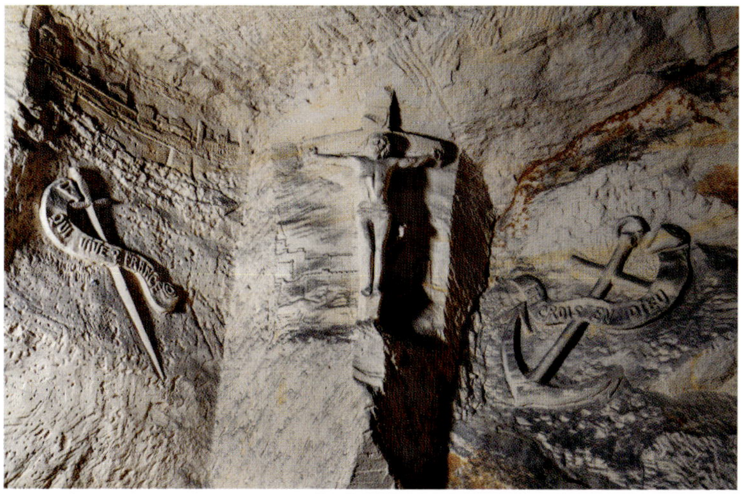

Six per cent of the 4,566 symbols logged in the Aisne and Oise battle areas had a religious reference.

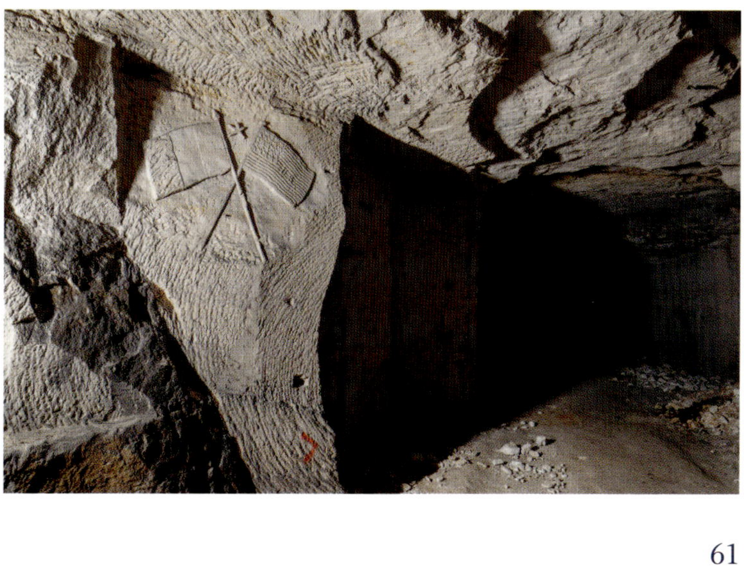

A French carving celebrating America joining the war – which heralded victory.

The Fighting Baritone

The quarries of Montigny some 100 kilometres north-east of Paris would make a splendid film set for an Indiana Jones sequel with their gigantic underground caverns and soaring pillars bursting with vegetation.

They supplied stone used in Baron Haussmann's nineteenth-century reconstruction of Paris and quarrying at the site dates back to the sixth century when its stone was used to make sarcophagi. Located near the village of Machemont in the Oise department, the caverns offered shelter for thousands of soldiers first from the French and then briefly the

Soaring pillars in the Montigny quarry at Machemont.

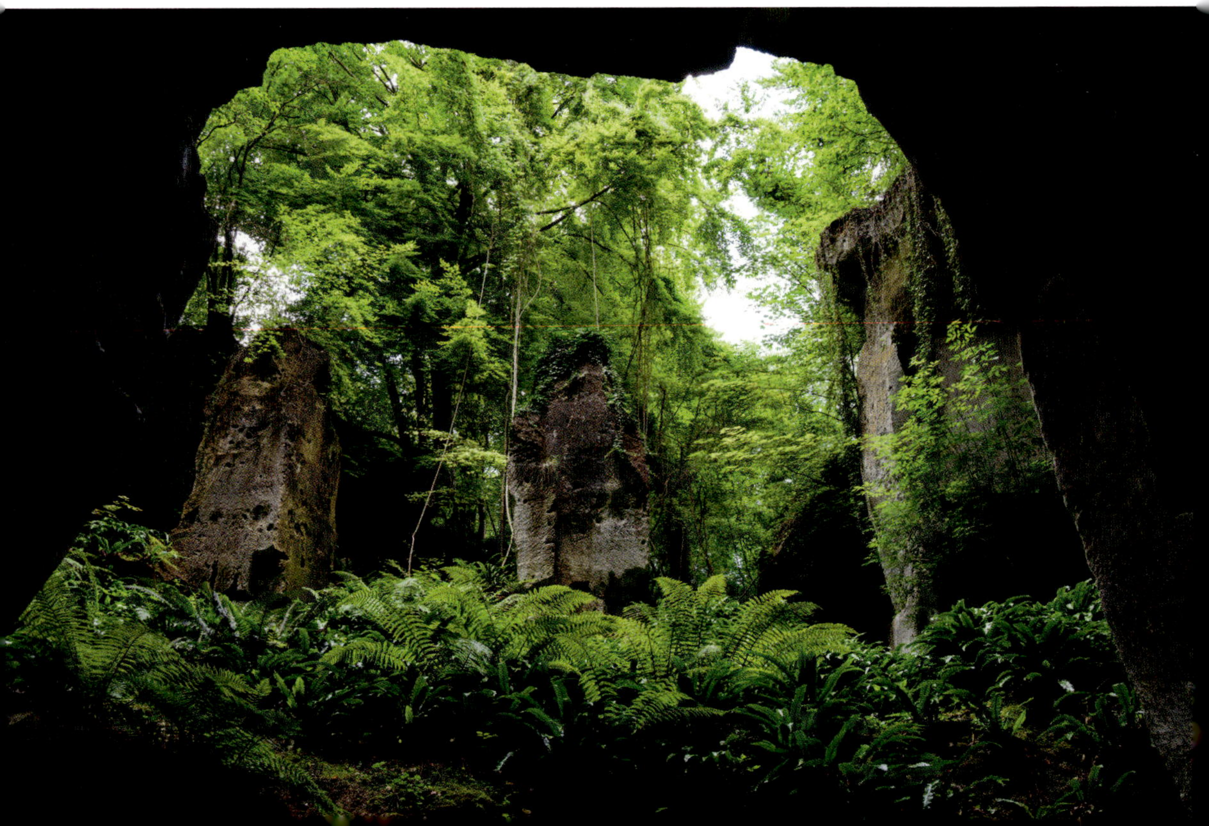

German armies. It was part of the front from September 1914 until March 1917 when the Germans withdrew to the Hindenburg Line of fortifications to shorten their line.

The quarries were a haven for rest and recuperation. They housed a field hospital, dormitories, kitchens and a stage for performances. Electric lighting was installed at the end of 1916 and the walls were covered with tar paper to insulate the caves from humidity. Walls were built to keep out poison gas and deep grooves can still be seen above entrances where airtight seals were fitted.

Like in other underground shelters, an altar was carved into the stone, but here, given the scale of the halls left by the stone-cutting, the atmosphere must have been more like that of a cathedral than a chapel.

On average, 500 soldiers occupied the quarry permanently, but the number doubled when the fighting intensified. The Germans took over the site several months into the 1918 Spring Offensive, but they held it for only two months until the French returned for good in mid-August.

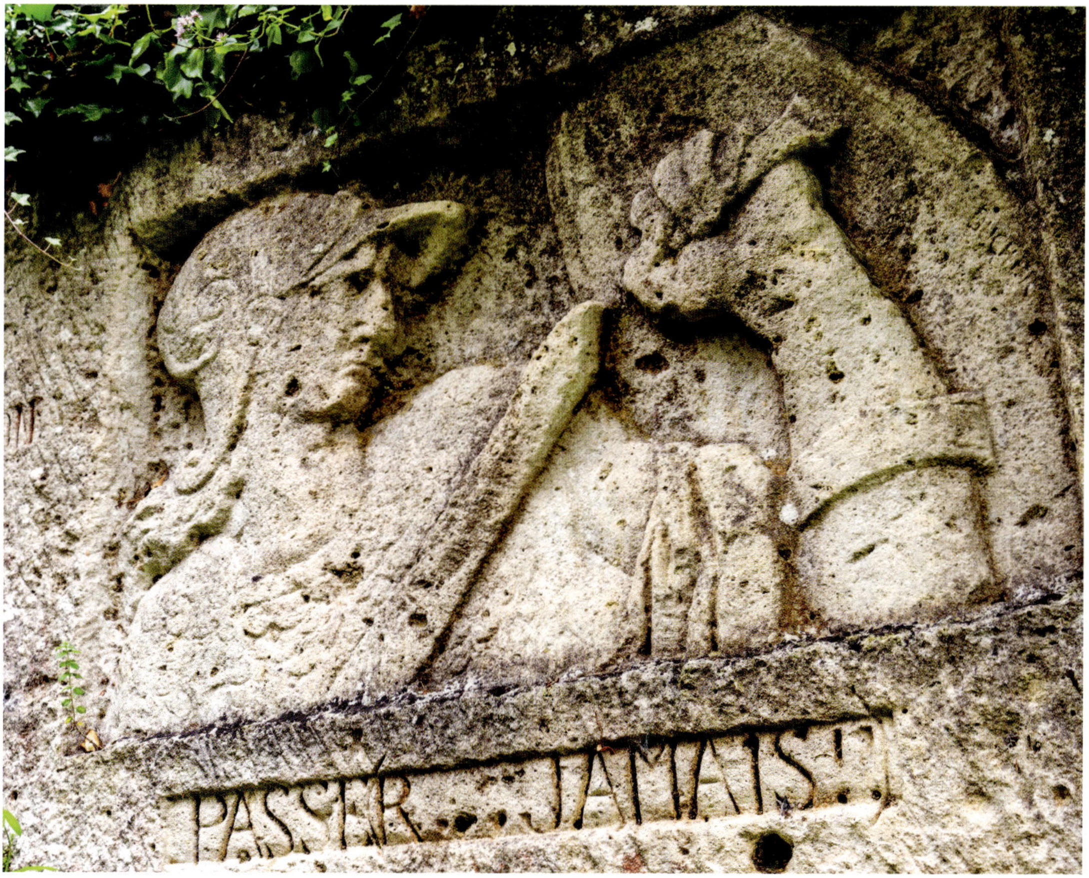

A work by the Swiss professional sculptor Edwin Bucher, who enlisted weeks after the outbreak of war and joined the Marching Regiment of the Foreign Legion (RMLE). The sculpture evokes the Greek goddess Athena and represents a defiant France defending herself. The inscription reads: 'Never Pass!'. Bucher survived the war.

More than fifteen French regiments, mainly from the infantry, were stationed at Montigny for prolonged periods during the four years of war.

The soldiers included Zouaves, an elite light infantry formation that had its origins in French North Africa in the nineteenth century. The Zouaves had a dashing uniform of baggy trousers, short open-fronted jacket and a fez-like cap, but they ditched the colour for regular khaki a few months into the war, for obvious reasons. Made up of both French nationals and North Africans, they were among the most decorated units of the war.

The bas-reliefs the soldiers cut into the stone on the outer walls and in the depths of the echoing labyrinth speak of patriotism, longing and hope.

The most prolific sculptor at Montigny was thirty-six-year-old Marius Cropait, an opera singer from the prestigious Opéra Comique in Paris who went by the stage name Marius Corpait and signed his rousing patriotic artworks accordingly.

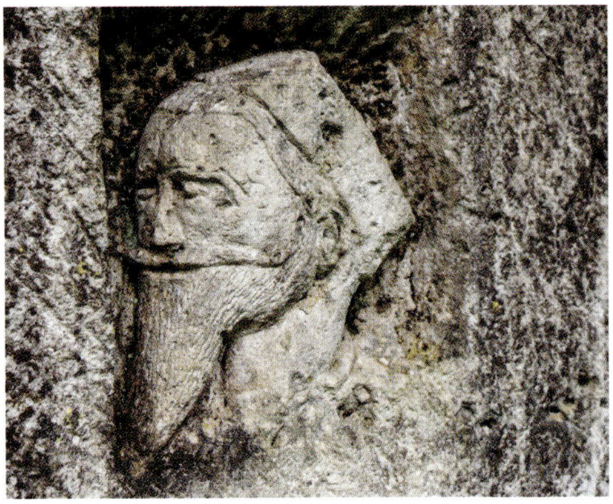

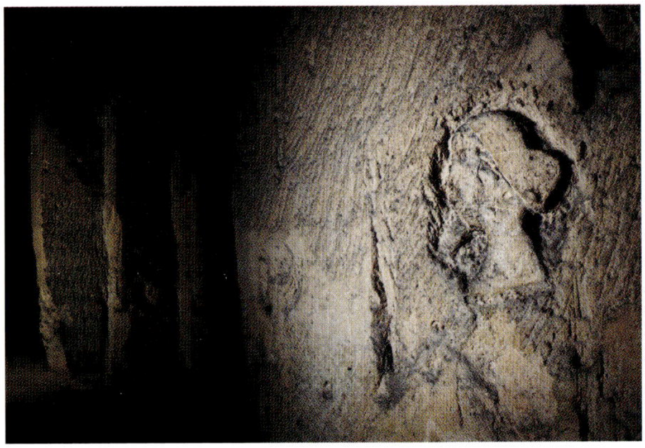

Above left: Carving of a Zouave soldier at Montigny.

Above right: A carving in the Montigny quarry.

Below left: The seven-flamed grenade emblem of the French Foreign Legion in the Montigny quarry.

Below right: Sculpture of a French officer wearing a gas mask pulled up on his forehead.

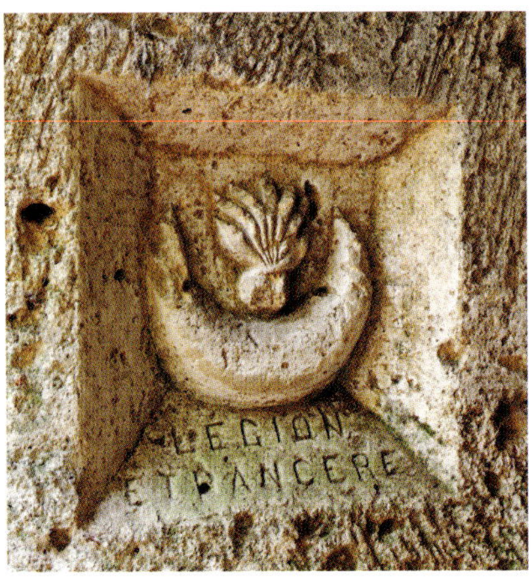

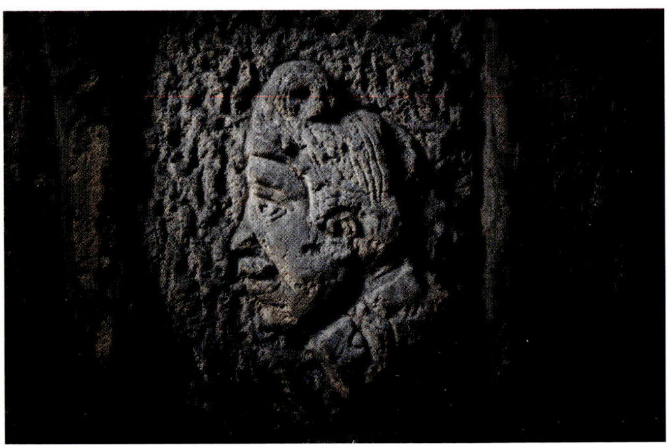

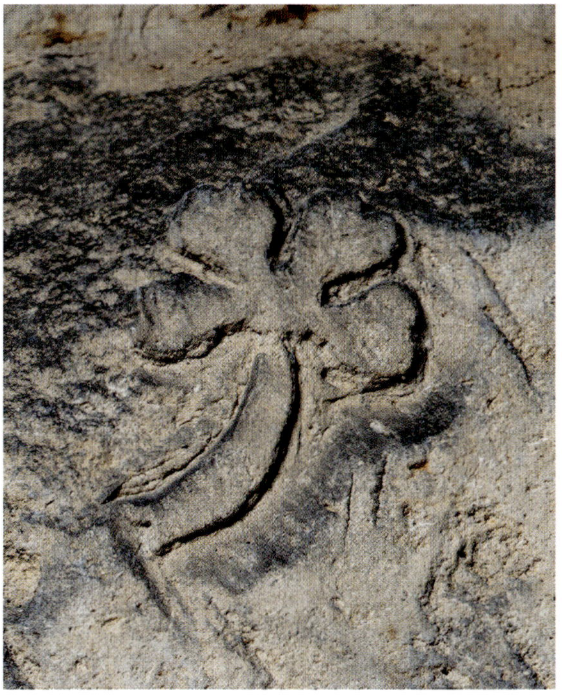

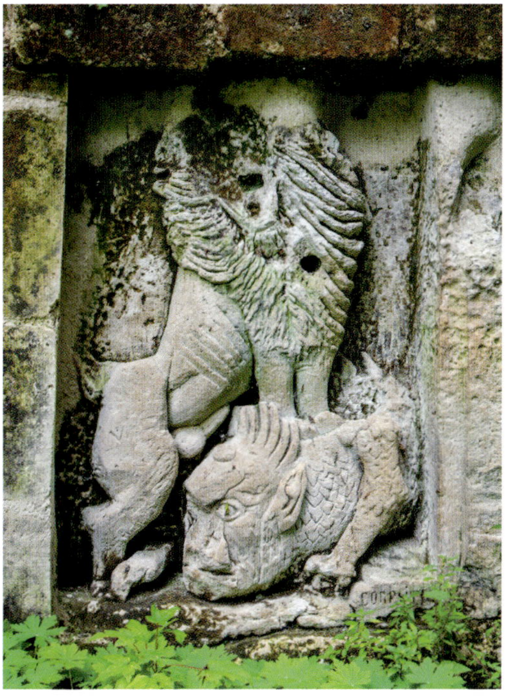

Above left: A four-leafed clover. A symbol of luck and hope.

Above right: Marius Corpait's sculpture of a French lion vanquishing the German monster.

They include a sculpture featuring a French lion, virile and indomitable, standing victorious with its two front legs on the back of a serpent-like monster with the face of the Kaiser, cruel, empty-eyed and snarling, a little spiked helmet pushed low over its forehead. The lion's face has disappeared, but the monster remains in reasonable condition, which is perhaps surprising given that the Kaiser's soldiers spent two months walking past it.

A few metres away, a more subtle work attributed to Corpait portrays Demeter, the Greek goddess of agriculture, or her Roman version Ceres. It appears to be modelled on the goddess that adorned the French 10 franc note in circulation at the time. In the context of the war and the destruction of French soil, the sculpture symbolises the harvests to come, after victory.

The holes in her breasts were probably used to hold candles to cast shadows on the body and the face but given that her genital area is also pierced there is also likely to have been a sexual connotation. Such holes were common in representations of the female form in underground quarries used by soldiers, and a crudely sculpted female torso just a few metres away from Demeter also features them.

Corpait had received some training in sculpture during his studies. He was no Michelangelo, but his work was nothing if not ambitious. The opera baritone had trained in the world-famous Paris Conservatory college of music and dance. He graduated with honours in 1905 and by the time war broke out, he was in the prime of his career, performing in leading roles in operas including *Romeo and Juliet, Samson and Delilah,* and *Carmen* in Paris, Bordeaux and Lyon. He had two daughters aged six and eleven.

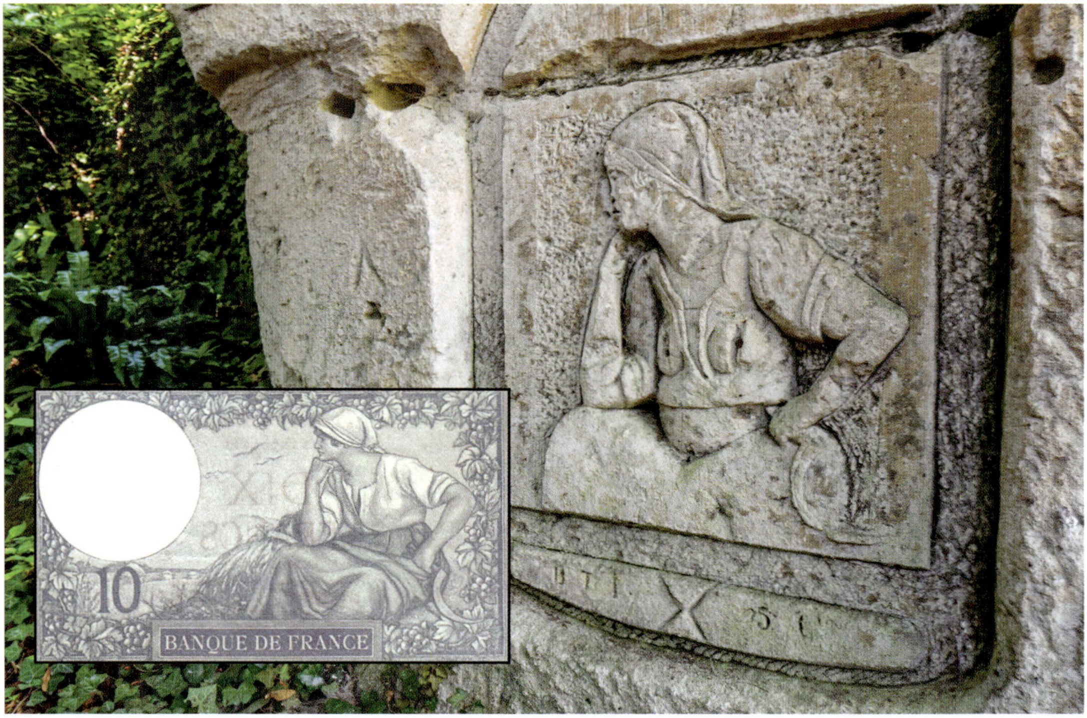

Above: The unsigned sculpture of the Greek goddess Demeter has been attributed to Marius Corpait. It was inspired by the French 10 franc note at the time.

Below left: Nude women are a common theme especially among French soldier artists.

Below right: Another example of sexual yearning left by French troops in a Chemin des Dames quarry.

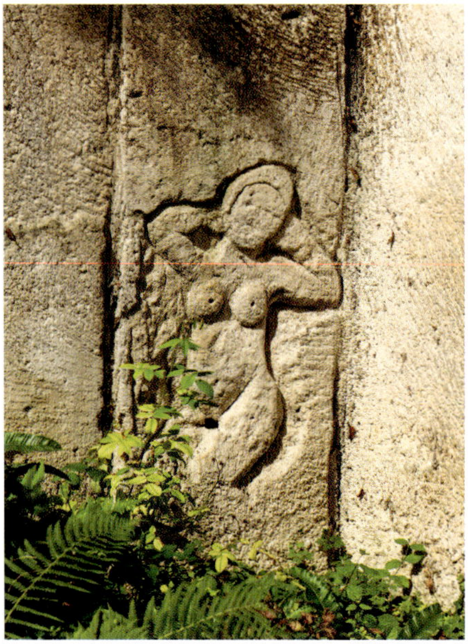

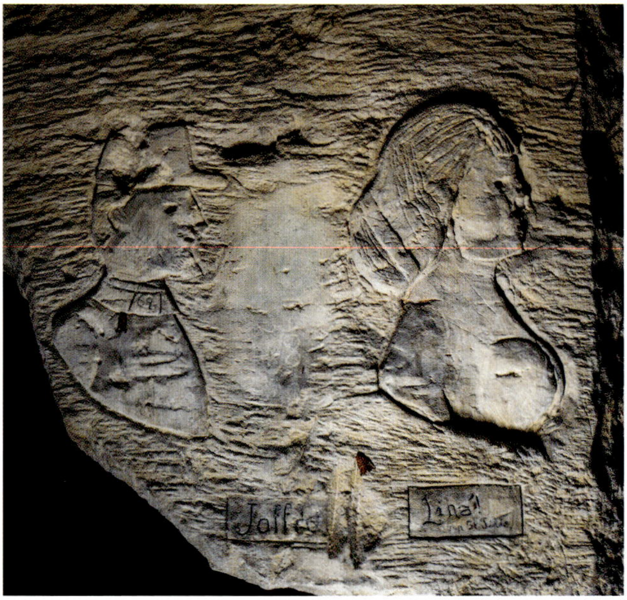

He didn't allow his plunge from the luxury and the beauty of the Paris stage to the hideous backdrop of the trenches shatter his spirit. He served in the French army for the entire four years of the war, the first two years as a private in the 11th Territorial Infantry Regiment, and won citations for courage and devotion to duty.

Corpait volunteered to join a special platoon charged with reconnaissance missions and the capture of prisoners. He was wounded in September 1914, sustaining multiple shrapnel wounds in the face. In between missions, he found time to create the sculptures to embellish the quarry and inspire the men.

After the war, he continued to perform in private recitals and ran a hotel restaurant in Maisons-Laffitte, a wealthy suburb of Paris, before becoming the proprietor of a cinema. He died in 1958 at the age of eighty-one.

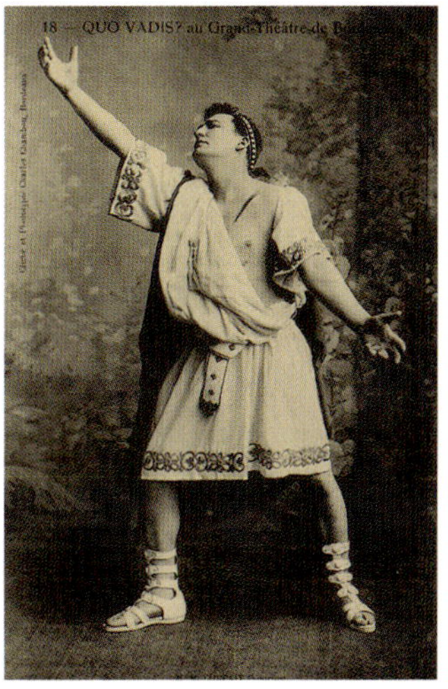

Right: Corpait performing in the opera *Quo Vadis* in the Bordeaux Grand Theatre before the war. (Bordeaux Municipal Library C.P. 5404)

Below left: Corpait and a faithful friend working on a bas-relief showing Nike, the winged goddess of victory, rising towards a rising sun and the outline of what appears to be a soldier hurling a grenade. (Courtesy of Bernard Lambot)

Below right: Corpait never finished the work, seen here in its condition today. He was transferred away from Montigny in December 1916.

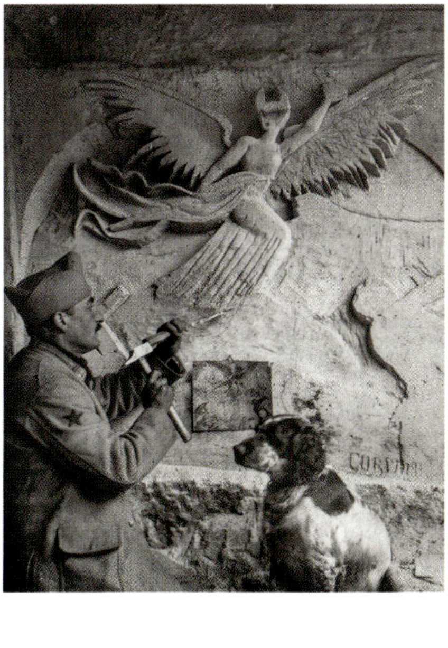

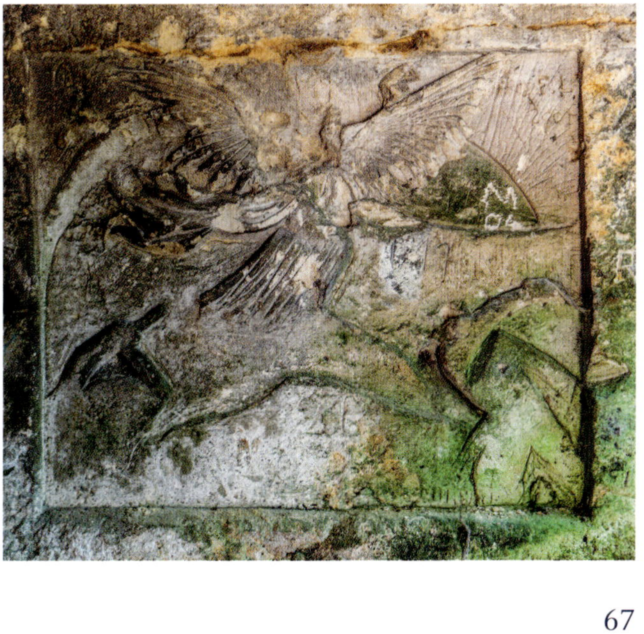

The Yankee Spirit

The US 26th Division was nicknamed the 'Yankee Division' because it was made up of National Guard troops from the six New England states. Most of them were volunteers, and many were relatively recent immigrants to the US from countries including Russia, Ukraine, Poland, Italy and Scotland. For them, in addition to being an adventure, military

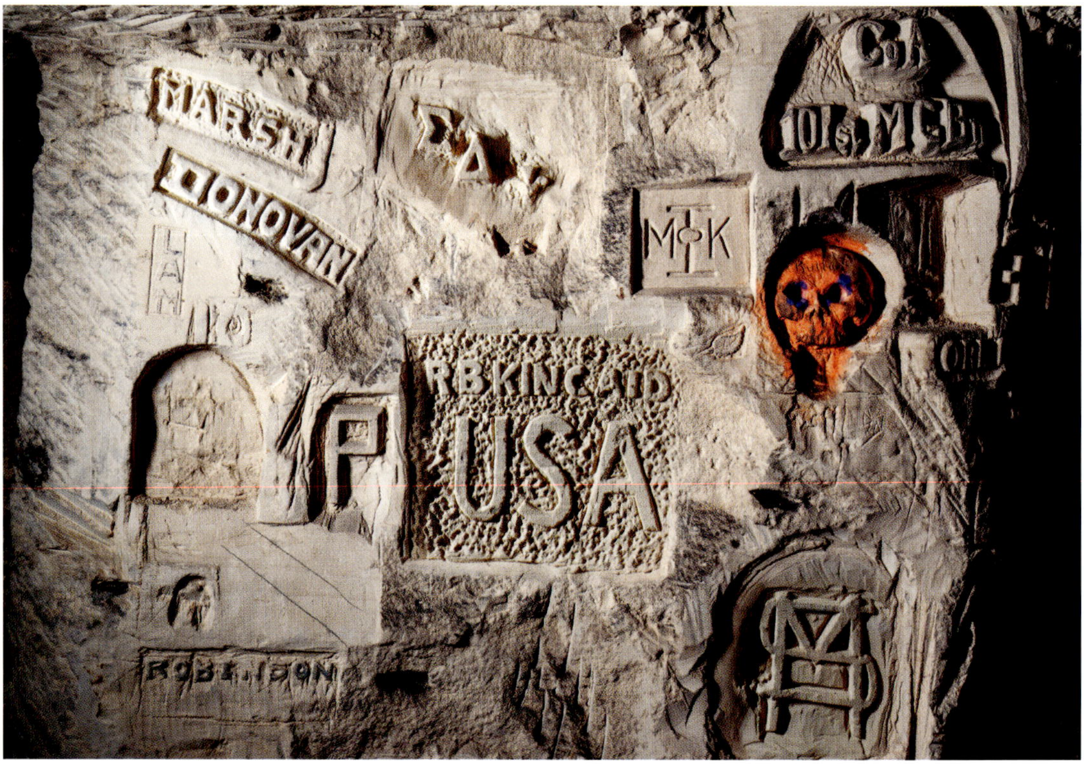

The Froidmont quarry has over 1,000 American inscriptions. They were made in just six weeks while soldiers of the 26th 'Yankee Division' sheltered here in early 1918.

service was an opportunity to show their loyalty to their new country – and to help out the homelands they came from.

Some units of the 26th dated back to the time of the Revolution. The nickname 'Doughboys' was a little younger – some historians believe it derives from the Mexican war of 1846–48 when American troops made long treks over dusty terrain, making them appear as though they were covered in flour, or dough.

During 1918 the American Expeditionary Force grew to an army of two million. It tipped the balance on the Western Front and after the failure of the German spring offensives in 1918, the realisation took hold in the German leadership that the war could not be won.

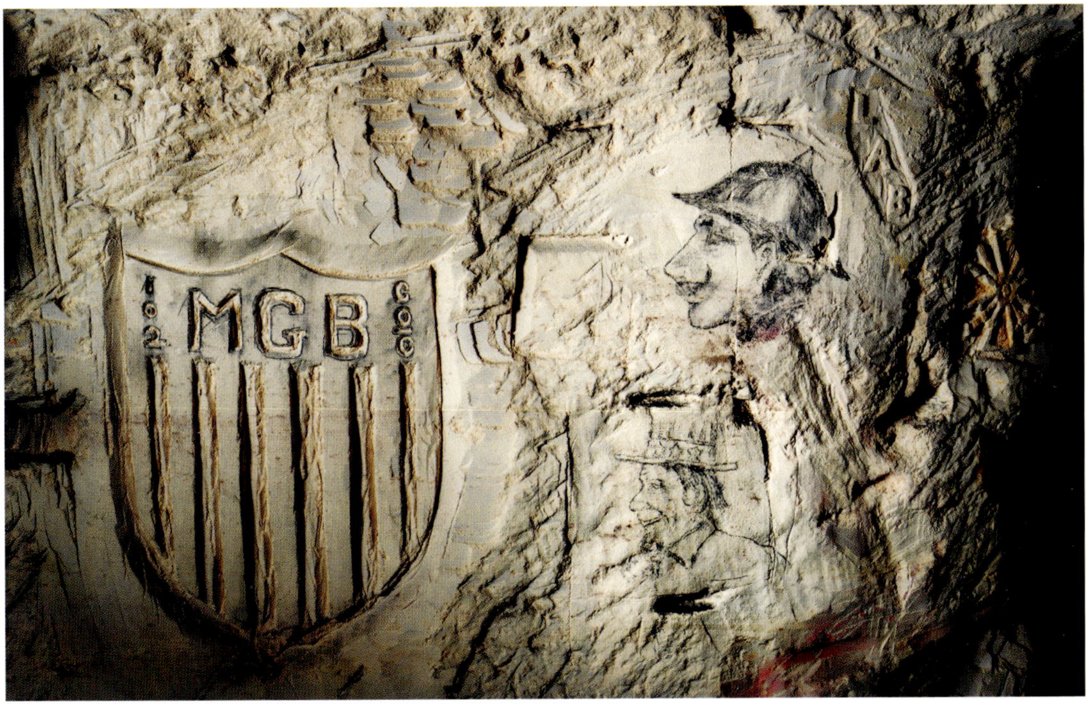

Above: A work dedicated to the 102nd Machine Gun Battalion (MGB) with drawings of Kaiser Wilhelm II wearing a Pickelhaube spiked helmet, and Uncle Sam beneath him.

Right: For God and USA.

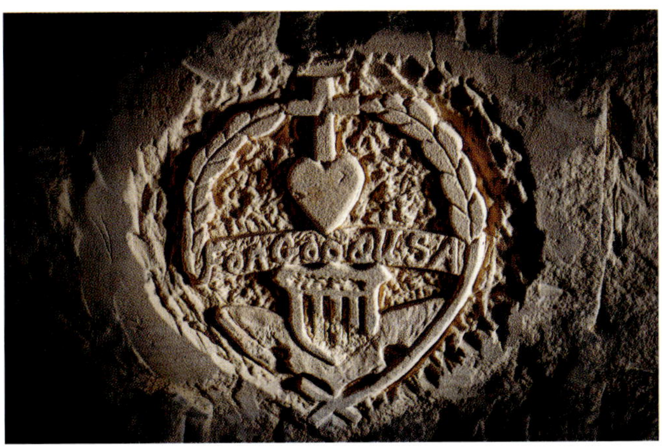

The newly arrived Doughboys were initially deployed along a relatively quiet part of the front line on the Chemin des Dames ridge. It was deemed a suitable place to give the untested Americans their baptism of fire – and to fill the gaps in the French line torn by the offensives in this sector in 1917.

The Yankees were placed under the command of a French general, Louis Ernest de Maud'huy, and French troops were seconded to instruct the Americans in the latest trench warfare tactics.

'It would never answer to have green hands left alone to face the tricks of foxy Fritz, and second, the Americans needed instruction which they could get in no other way,' wrote Frank Sibley, a reporter for the Boston Globe who was embedded with the Yankees. 'Their officers were courteous as only French officers can be, patient with our mistakes – and if they were re amused by some of our ways, they concealed it from us.'

Raring for action, the Americans broke an informal truce between the battle-worn French and German troops on the Chemin des Dames, firing at anything that moved, according to the American military historian Jonathan Bratten, who cited a division history as saying the Americans turned 'no man's land into Yankee land.'

Inexperienced they may have been – but within just a few months, they were proving more than a match for seasoned German stormtroopers.

During their apprenticeship, the Yankees found shelter in quarries such as Froidmont. The labyrinth, big enough to accommodate hundreds of men, had been occupied by

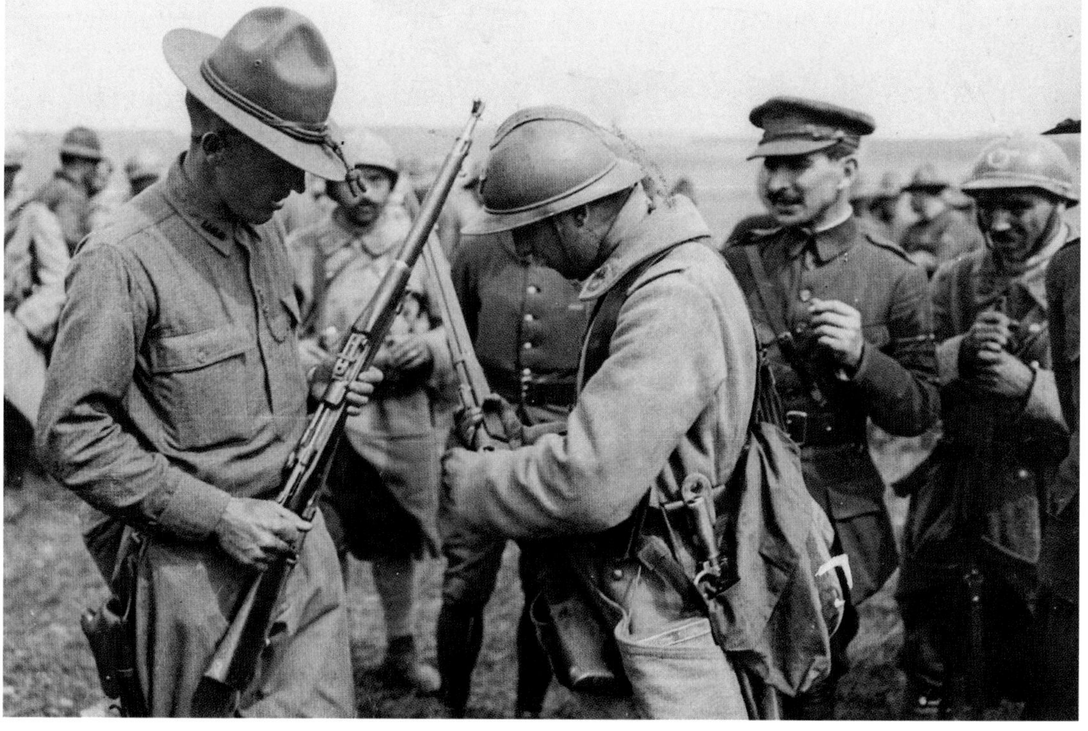

US soldiers undergoing instruction from French soldiers at Houdelaincourt, July 1917. (La Contemporaine VAL 225/110 Producer: Section photographique de l'armée)

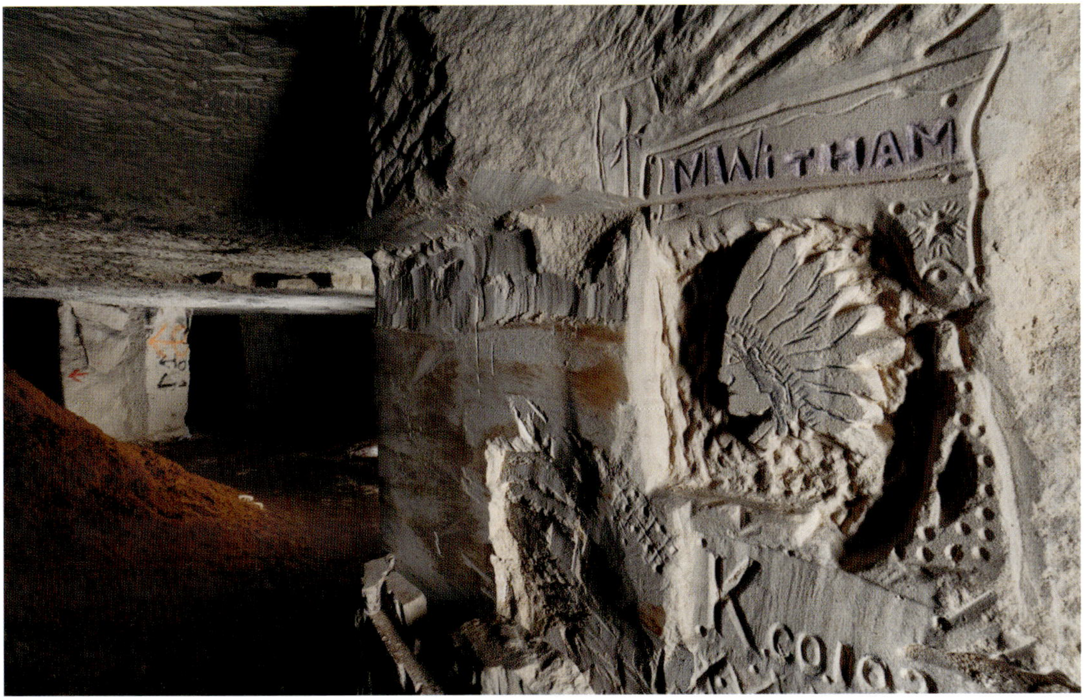

Above: Carvings of native American profiles with headdresses were a popular theme among US soldiers adorning the walls with symbols of their country.

Right: This carving evokes Sitting Bull.

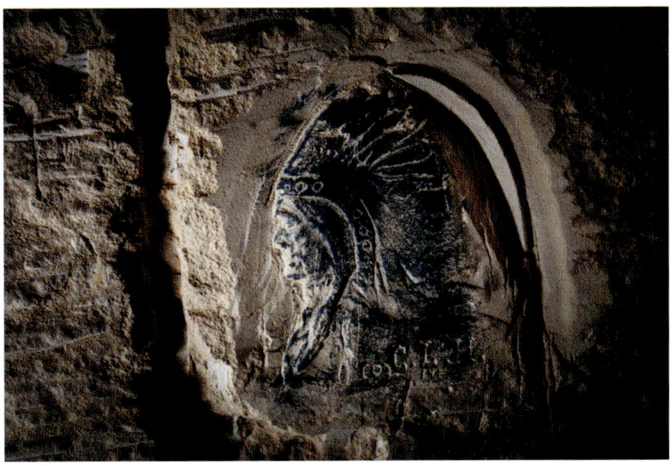

German troops from September 1914 until they were taken over by the French in late October 1917. The Yankees were in Froidmont for just six weeks, in February and March 1918, and created a wealth of carvings that to this day pulsate with the exuberance of fresh troops. Subjects include national symbols such as Buffalo Bill and Native Americans with feather headdresses, as well as the Square and Compasses that reflects the popularity of the Freemasons and other fraternities in the United States at the time. Many of the names hewn into the rock are crafted in big and bold letters that, despite the massive German offensive yet to come, seem to augur the Allied victory.

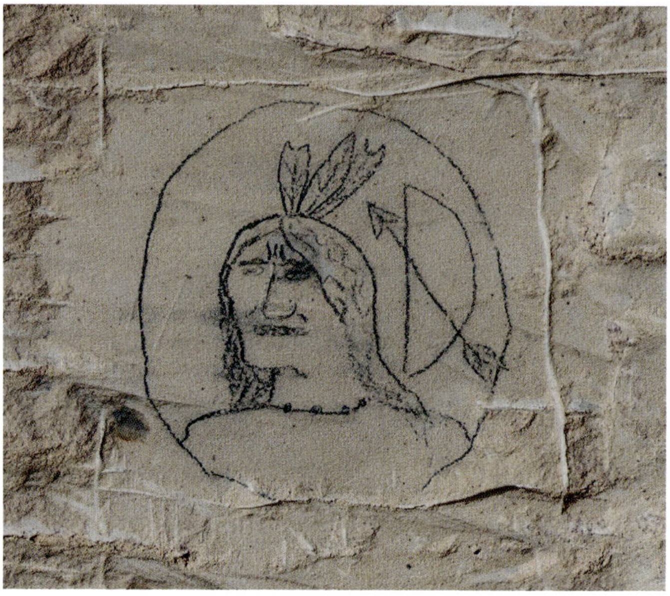

Soldiers from the Passamaquoddy people served in Company I of the 103rd Infantry Regiment of the Yankee Division, but it is unclear whether native Americans left traces at Froidmont.

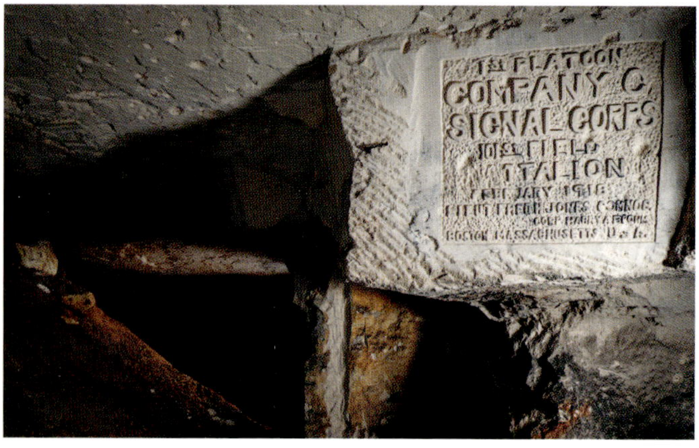

A panel crafted by members of a Signal Corps platoon from Boston, Massachusetts.

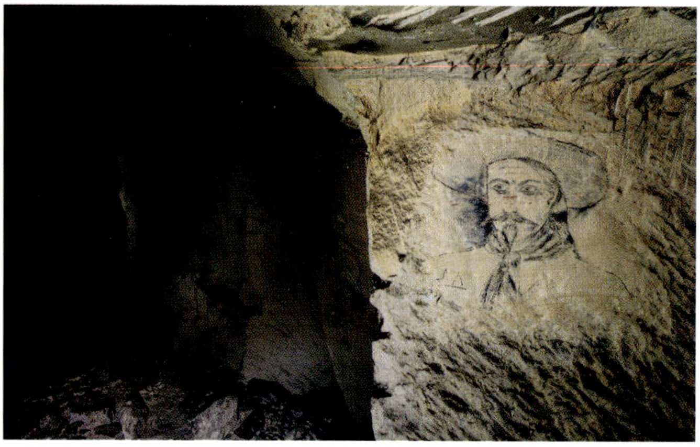

Buffalo Bill also served as a national symbol.

Archie Sweetman of the 101st Regiment carved a portrait of himself in profile above his name, 'Sweetman of South Boston,' which is written in pencil and barely legible now. He was wounded in a gas attack on 22 July 1918, but he survived and became an artist after the war. He was selected by the US Navy to create an official painting of the warship USS Constitution. He graduated from the Massachusetts College of Art in Boston in 1993 at the age of ninety-eight and lived to be a hundred years old.

Ralph T. Moan from Maine, who left his name in another Yankee-occupied quarry near Froidmont, kept a diary that conveyed the excitement shared by many American soldiers at the prospect of getting into the fight, in stark contrast with the Europeans at that time, exhausted by more than three years of carnage.

Moan arrived in France in late October 1917. The first few months were spent on drill including 14-mile marches and guard duty. In the first weeks of 1918 his unit got ever closer to the war. They arrived in the destroyed French town of Soissons, some 100 kilometres north-east of Paris, in February 1918: '...it sure was some interesting place for the Germans

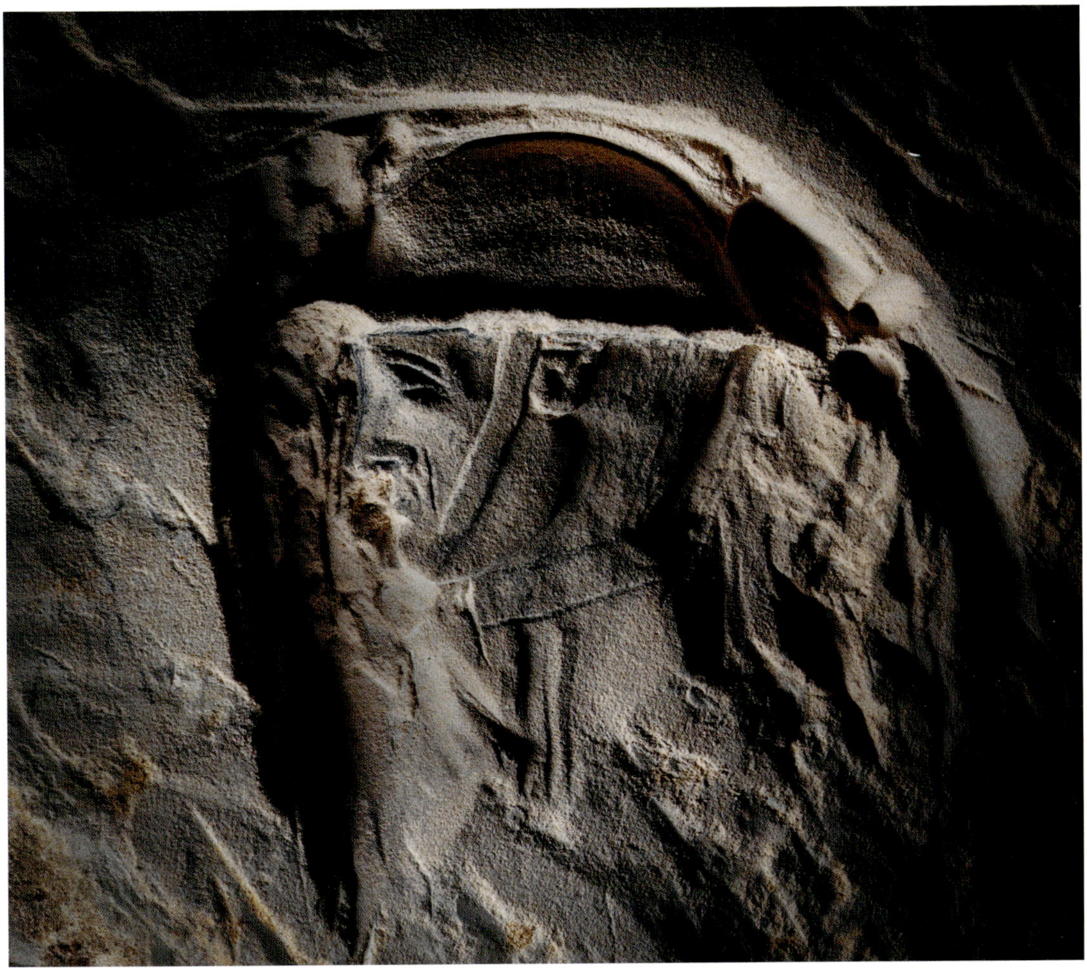

The self-portrait of Archie Sweetman of the 101st Regiment.

had once been within two miles of it and had bombarded practically everything to pieces with heavy artillery fire,' wrote Moan.

He set about souvenir-hunting, a dangerous pastime eschewed by the French because the Germans had a habit of boobytrapping tempting artefacts like helmets.

But soon, even Moan was sounding less enthusiastic. On 17 February, a sunny day, he witnessed a dogfight between German and French planes. One of the three 'Boche

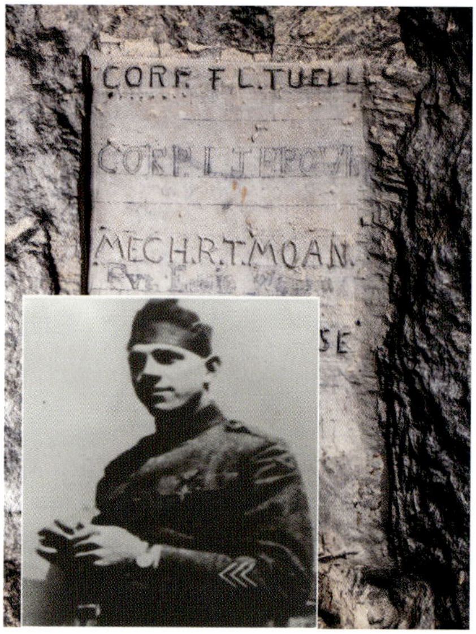

Left: The carving made by Ralph T. Moan, from Maine, in a quarry near the Chemin des Dames. The inset photo shows the soldier who started writing a war diary – but stopped after a few weeks of combat.

Below: An American carving depicting a woman chained to a post being threatened by the German soldier behind her. There is an American flag to her left and the woman, described in pencil as 'Little Matrony,' declares 'You my hope they get out.' The work is signed Michael Kobylanski.

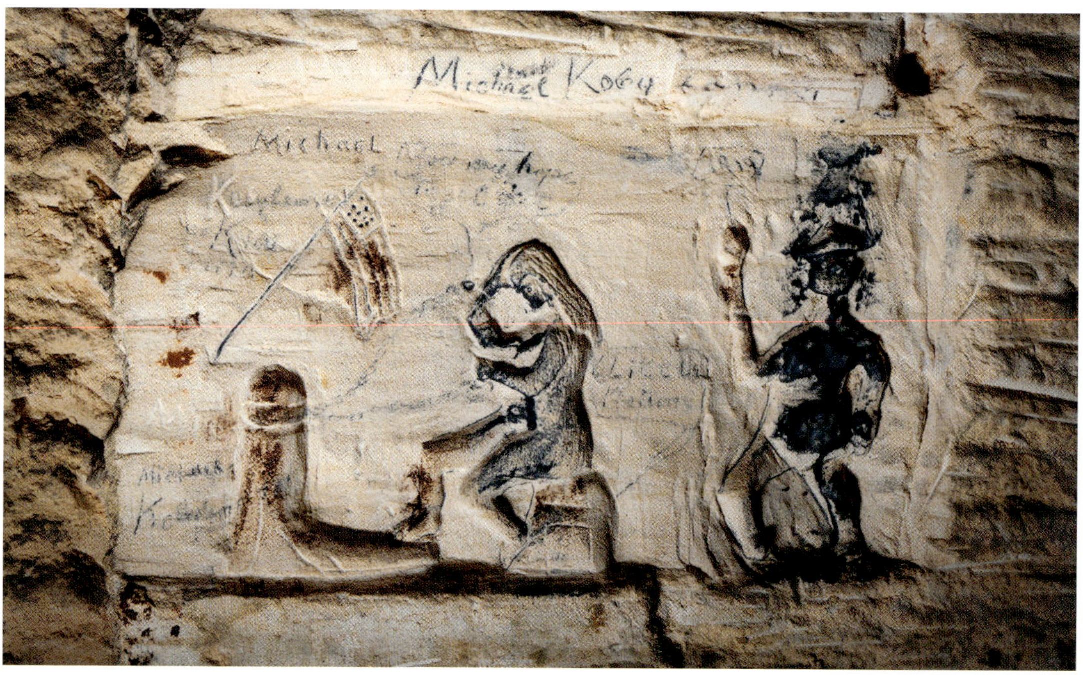

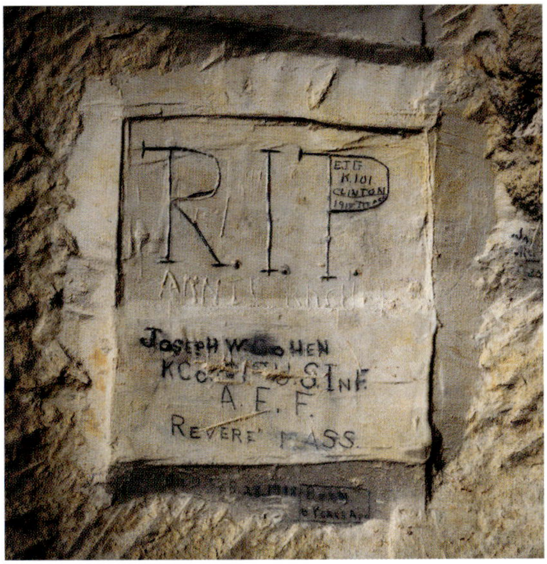

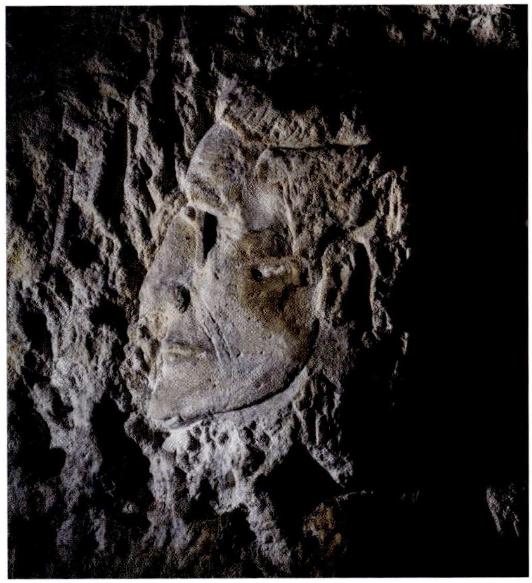

Above left: An American soldier's dedication to a fallen comrade at the Rouge-Maison quarry.

Above right: A rendition of the American President Woodrow Wilson in a quarry near the Chemin des Dames used by the 103rd Infantry Regiment of the Yankee Division.

machines' fell out of the sky in a streak of fire. They ran over to the crash site. 'The two Boche were no fit sight for a nervous man to look at. They were all in a pulp, jelly form and one man's head was driven way down into his chest.'

A few days later, his unit moved a few miles closer to the front and came under bombardment.

'I will never forget the peculiar feeling in my stomach when I heard the first heavy shell whistling over my head. You could hear the gun go off in the German line then the whistling of the shell and finally the explosion,' wrote Moan.

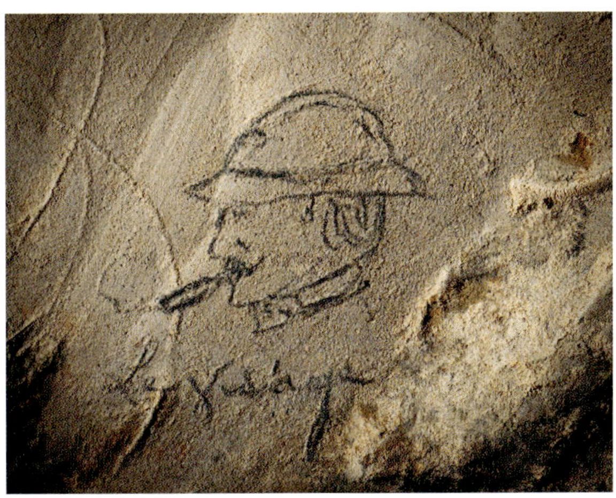

'Le visage' – a profile of a French officer.

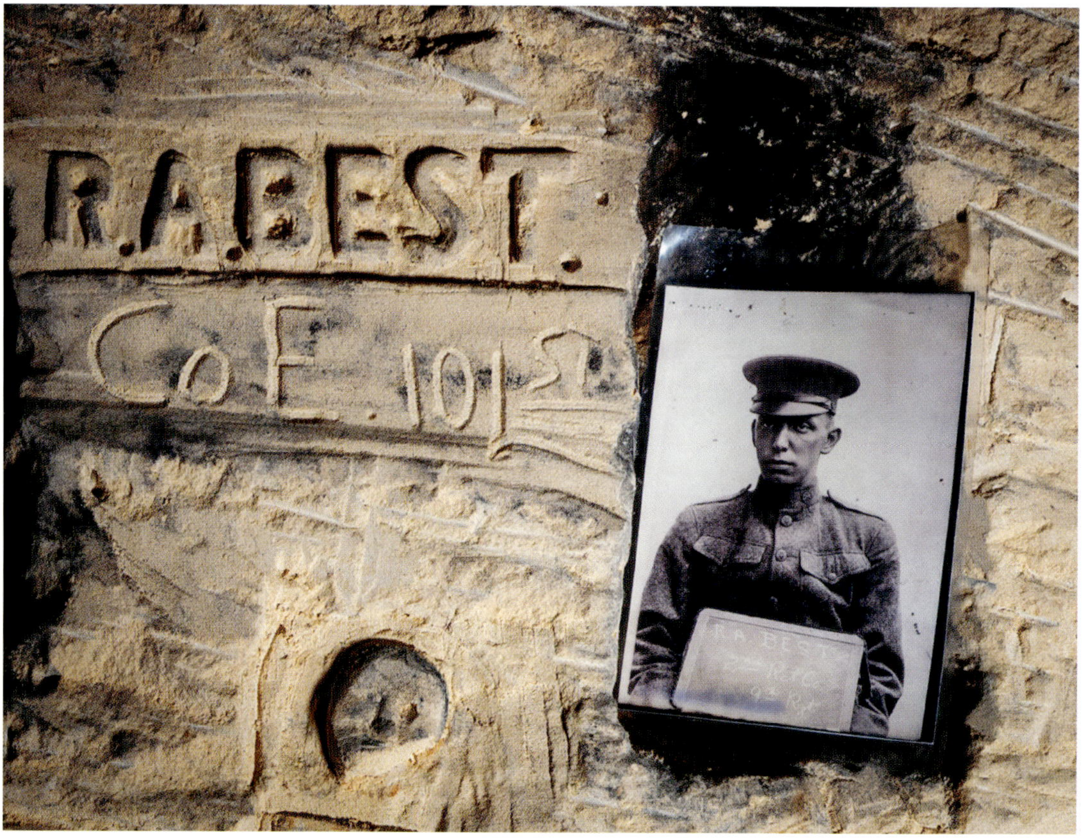

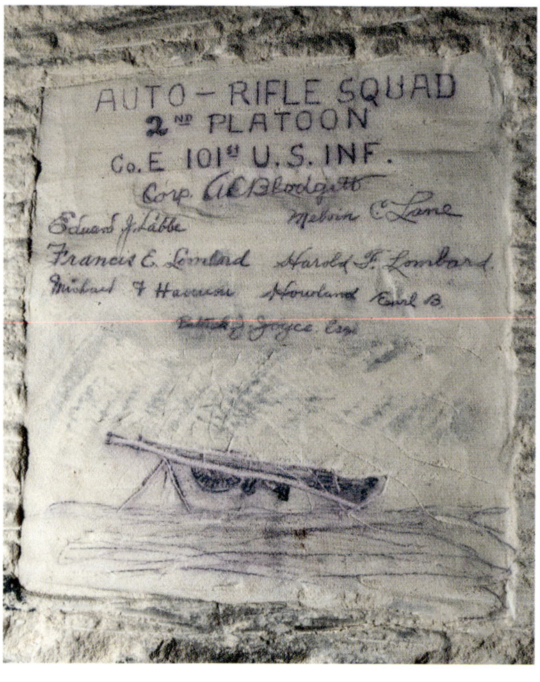

Above: Robert A. Best, a Canadian immigrant to the US, was last seen alive on 23 October 1918.

Left: Many of the American inscriptions are still in good condition.

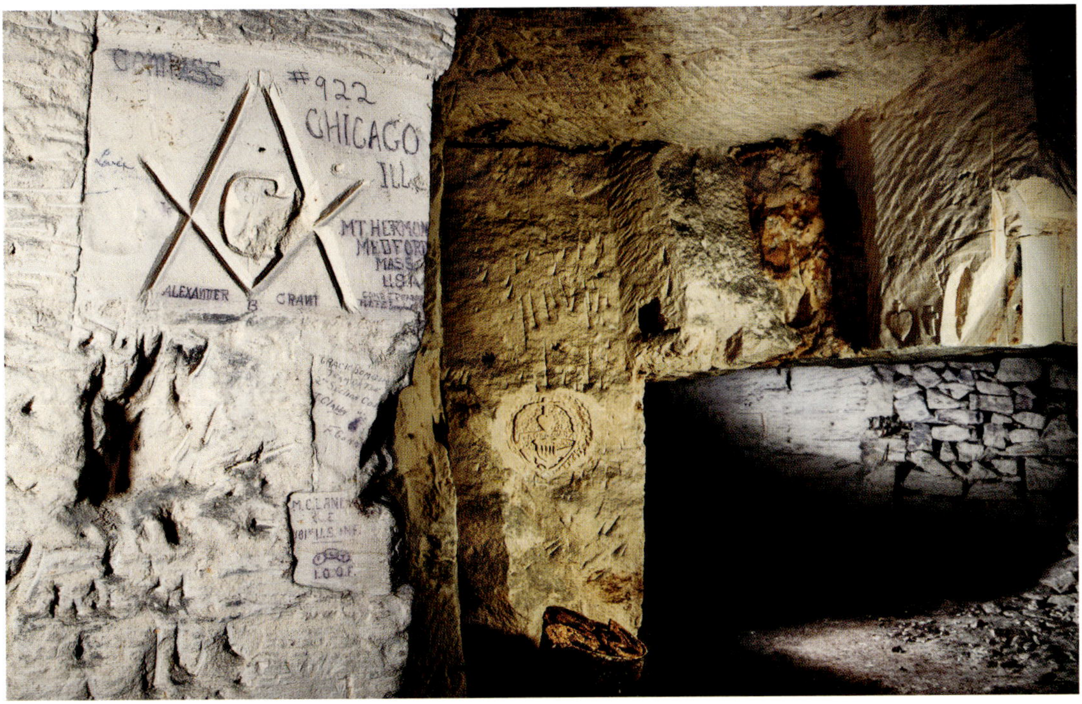

The large number of Masonic symbols carved into the walls reflects the popularity of Freemasonry and other fraternal organisations in the US at the time. Private Alexander B. Grant of the 101st Infantry was killed on 30 October 1918.

On 6 March, his unit arrived in the first-line trench and he was awakened the next morning by a big shell exploding directly over his dugout. 'The Boche bombarded us in good shape, at least seventy big fellows bursting every minute. Believe me, the man who said he was not scared is a liar.'

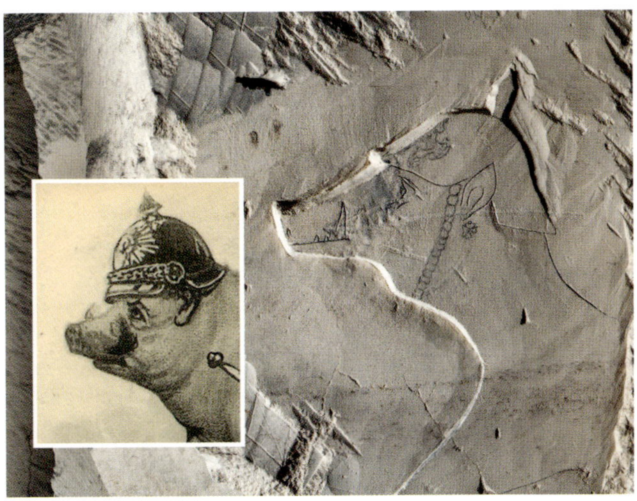

A carving attributed to an American soldier, possibly inspired by propaganda cartoons such as the inset photo portraying Kaiser Wilhelm II as a pig wearing a Pickelhaube spiked helmet.

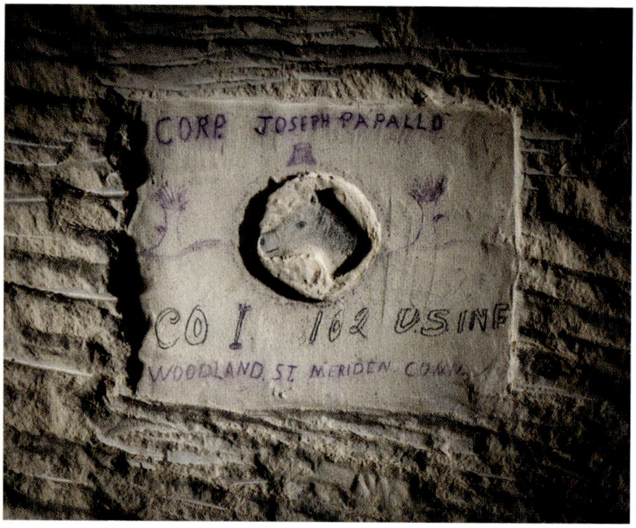

Left: The work of John Papallo from Connecticut, a corporal in the 102nd US Infantry Regiment. He was an immigrant from the Italian region of Calabria. Historians believe the two trees were a reference to the Charter Oak on Wyllys Hyll in Hartford, Connecticut, a symbol of American independence.

Below: References to the opposite sex by US Soldiers were considerably more restrained than among French soldiers.

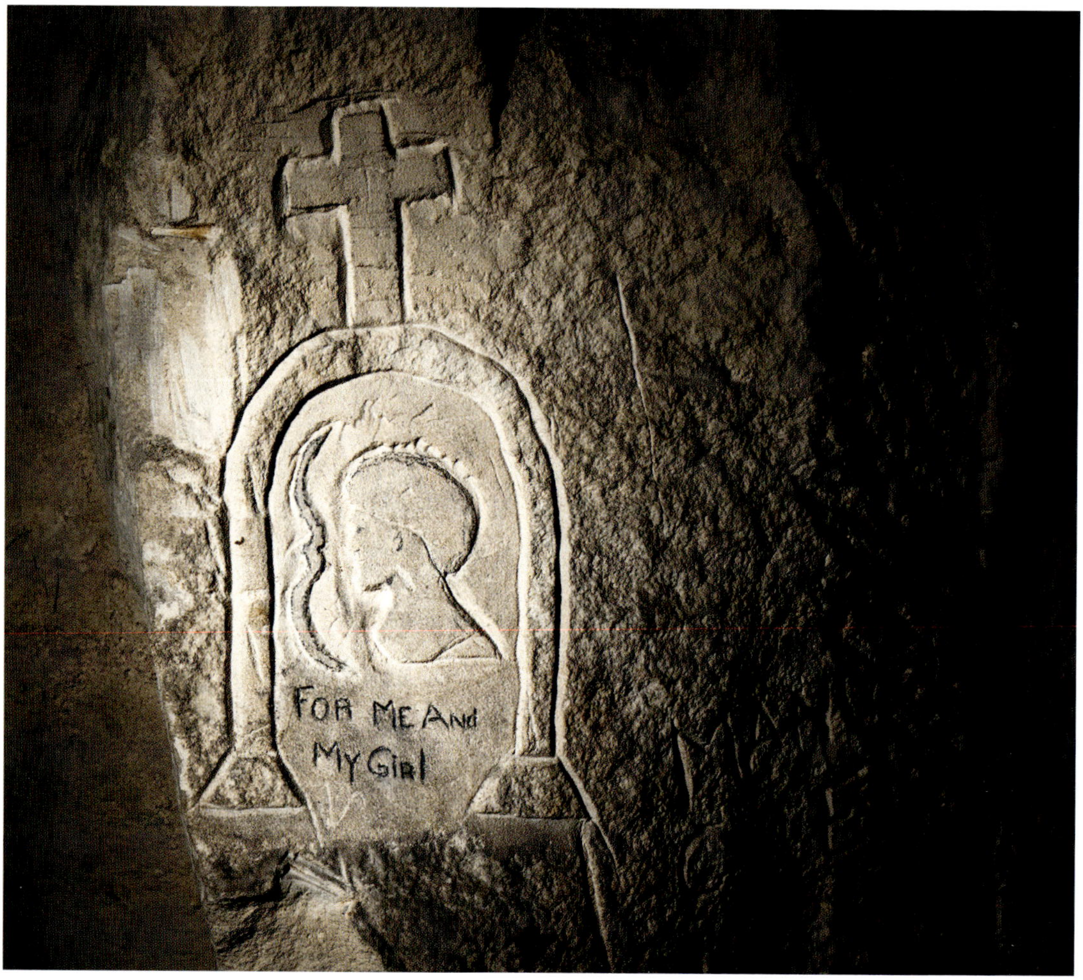

Over a century on, many of the inscriptions at Froidmont look as fresh as if the Yankees had only just left. Known locally as the 'Creute des Yankees' ('Yankee Cave'), it is guarded and maintained by the Chemin des Dames Association, a heritage society set up to research and preserve the historic site. The group has sealed off the entrances to keep out intruders who had been raiding the quarry for souvenirs. Its president, Gilles Chauwin, led me through a trap door and down two vertical ladders into the labyrinth.

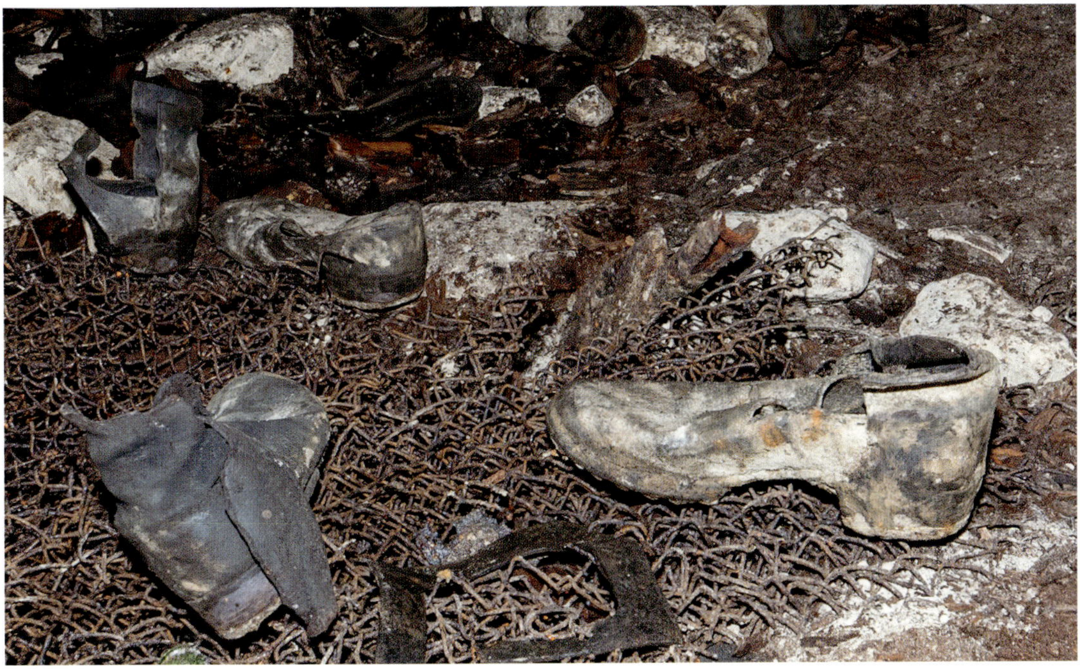

Above: Discarded boots at Froidmont.

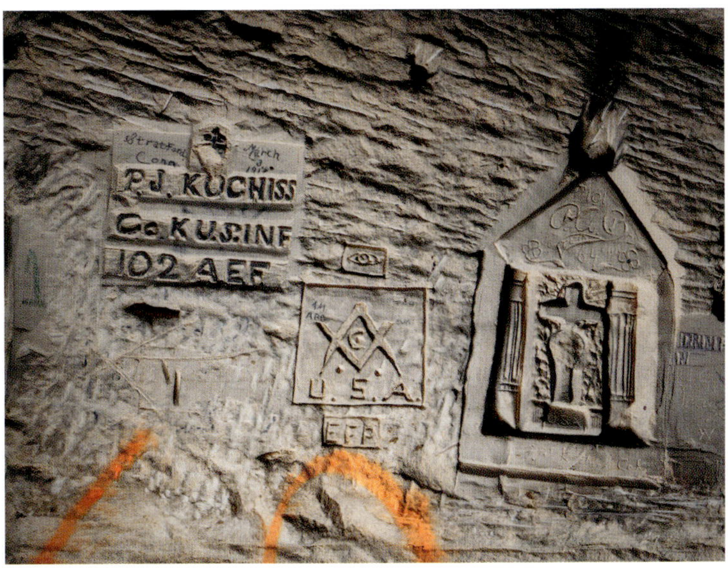

Right: Peter John Kochiss, the son of Slovak immigrants, was killed in action on 23 October 1918 – nineteen days before the end of the war.

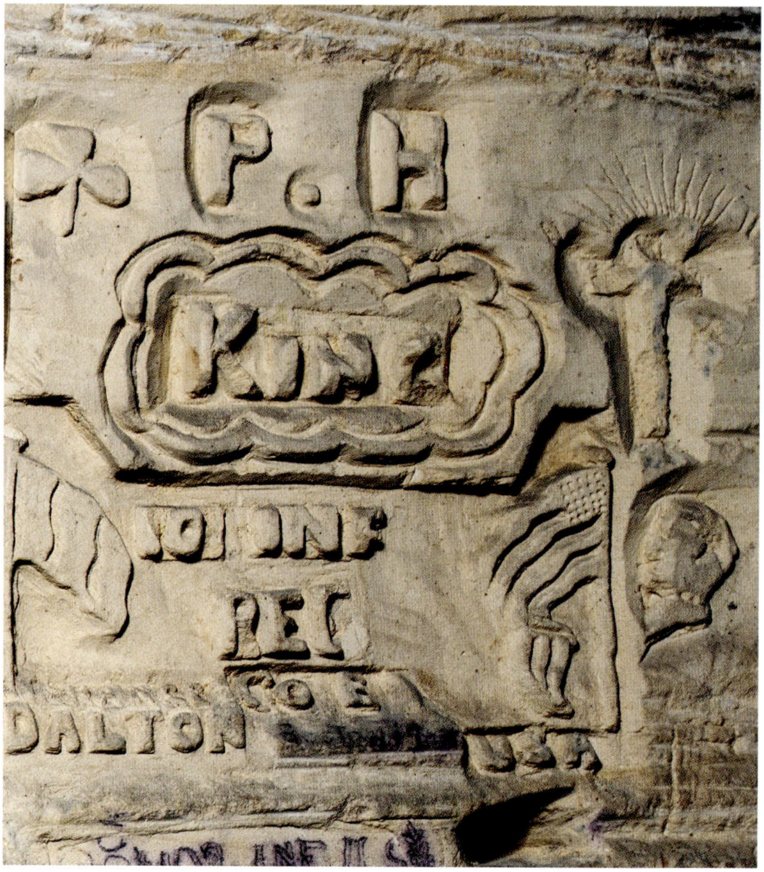

P.H. King of the 101st Infantry Regiment carved a shamrock to denote his Irish origin, the French and US flags and a cross with sunrays. The profile at the bottom right could be General John Pershing, the commander of the American Expeditionary Force.

We walked across uneven ground, bending down to avoid low sections of ceiling, past rusted shell casings, helmets and the skeletons of rifles, machine gun magazines and rolls of barbed wire.

Captain Daniel W. Strickland of the 26th Division's 102nd Infantry Regiment described how it was in February 1918 in his history *Connecticut Fights*:

> The caverns were long, wide, winding tunnels, and broad well lighted chambers hewn out of the soft stone, where the light and shadow effect of thousands of soldiers coming and going back and forth with glimmering candles and electric torches reminded one of the tales from Arabian Nights. Here and there the cigarettes glowed from shadowy corners or bunks, like fireflies on a summer night. One could wander through the intricate maze of passages and chambers for miles, sometimes coming upon groups of the French, surprising them with the American khaki.

In an illustration of how enemy soldiers respected each other's graffiti, Pierre Theoleyre of the French 72nd Infantry Regiment neatly pencilled his name in 1917, 5 centimetres away from the inscription left by W. Schmitz of the 161st Regiment to mark his nine-day stay in the quarry in July 1915.

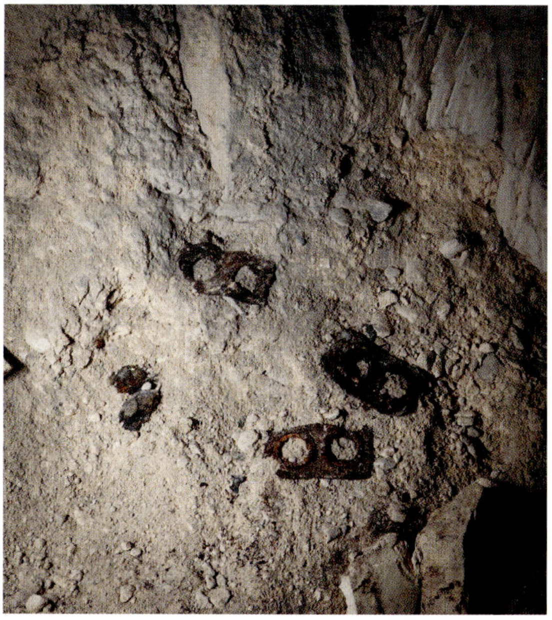

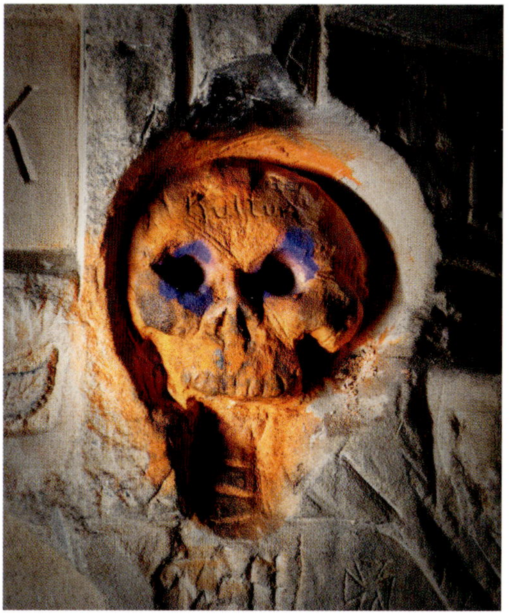

Above left: Remains of gas masks at Froidmont.

Above right: Another rare example of enmity: this American carving has the words 'Boche Kultur' inscribed on the forehead. Boche was used as a pejorative term for Germans.

Below: Enemy soldiers respected each other's traces, as these French and German inscriptions show.

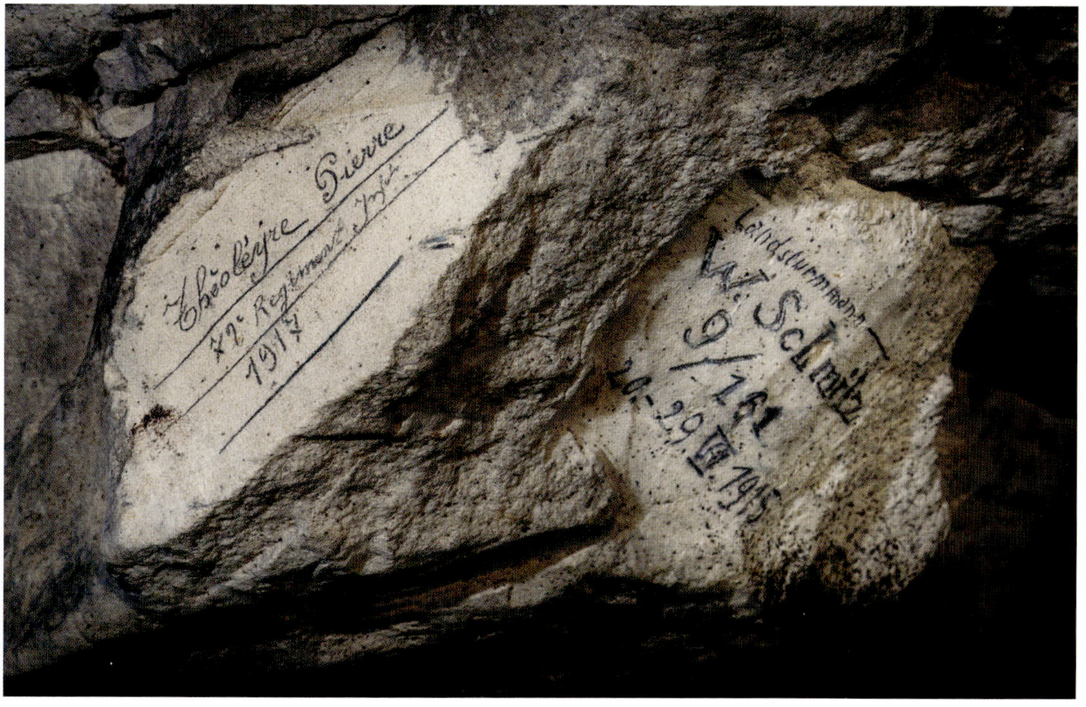

Chauwin said that despite the differences in the inscriptions made by the Germans, French and Americans at Froidmont, they all had the same reasons for making their mark on the walls:

> They had to keep themselves occupied at night ahead of an attack or during a bombardment. If you don't occupy your spirit you go mad, it is a way of mentally escaping the horror. Also, they all shared the fear of death. And they all wanted to show 'I was here, I participated in something extraordinary, I did my job.' No one wants to be forgotten. They were worried not just about dying, but about literally disappearing at any time, being obliterated by a shell so that there would be nothing left of them. These inscriptions are like bottles thrown into the sea.

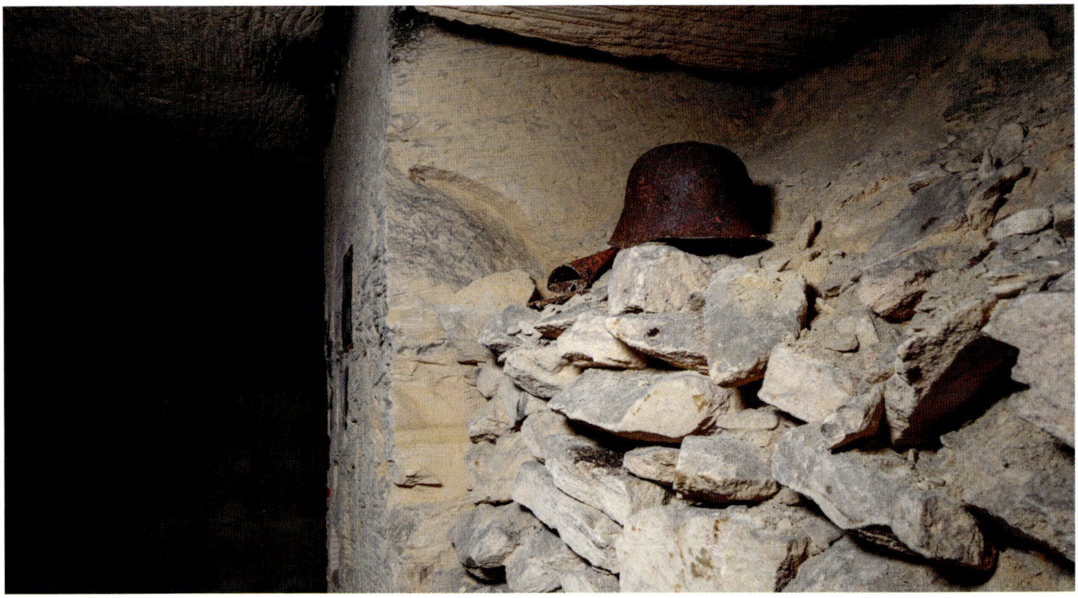

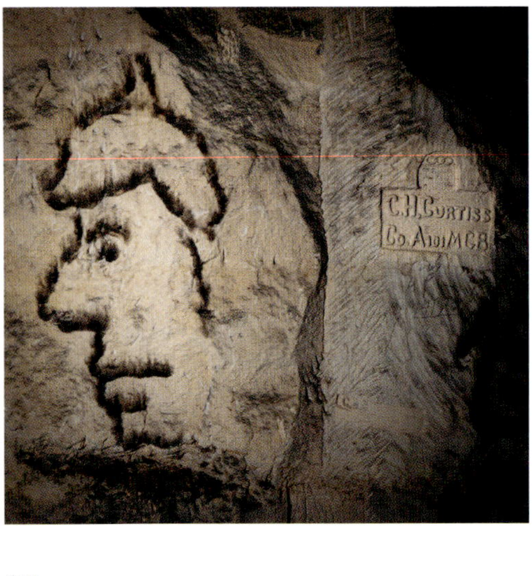

Above: A German helmet at Froidmont.

Left: C.H. Curtiss of the 101st Machine Gun Battalion was a member of the Independent Order of Odd Fellows. (IOOF)

On the night of 11 March, the second platoon of Moan's company spotted a German patrol and attacked them with hand grenades and machine guns. 'They laid up twenty that night and left them hanging in the wire. One man had his head blown off and it made a ghastly sight, suspended in the barbed wire.'

Moan had seen enough. 'Have decided to cut this diary out right now, for no man wishes after seeing what we have seen to recall them but rather wishes to forget,' he wrote on 30 March 1918. 'From now on all we see is HELL.'

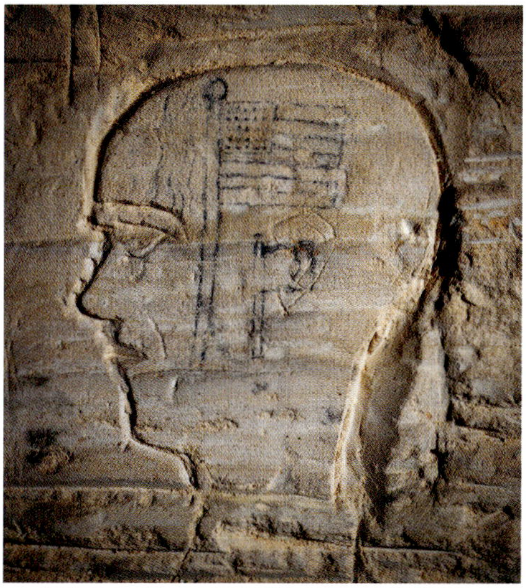

Right: Even though many inscriptions reflect patriotic sentiment. more than twice as many express attachment to a military unit such as a regiment or battalion.

Below: The initial exuberance of the American Expeditionary Force was tempered soon after their arrival in France.

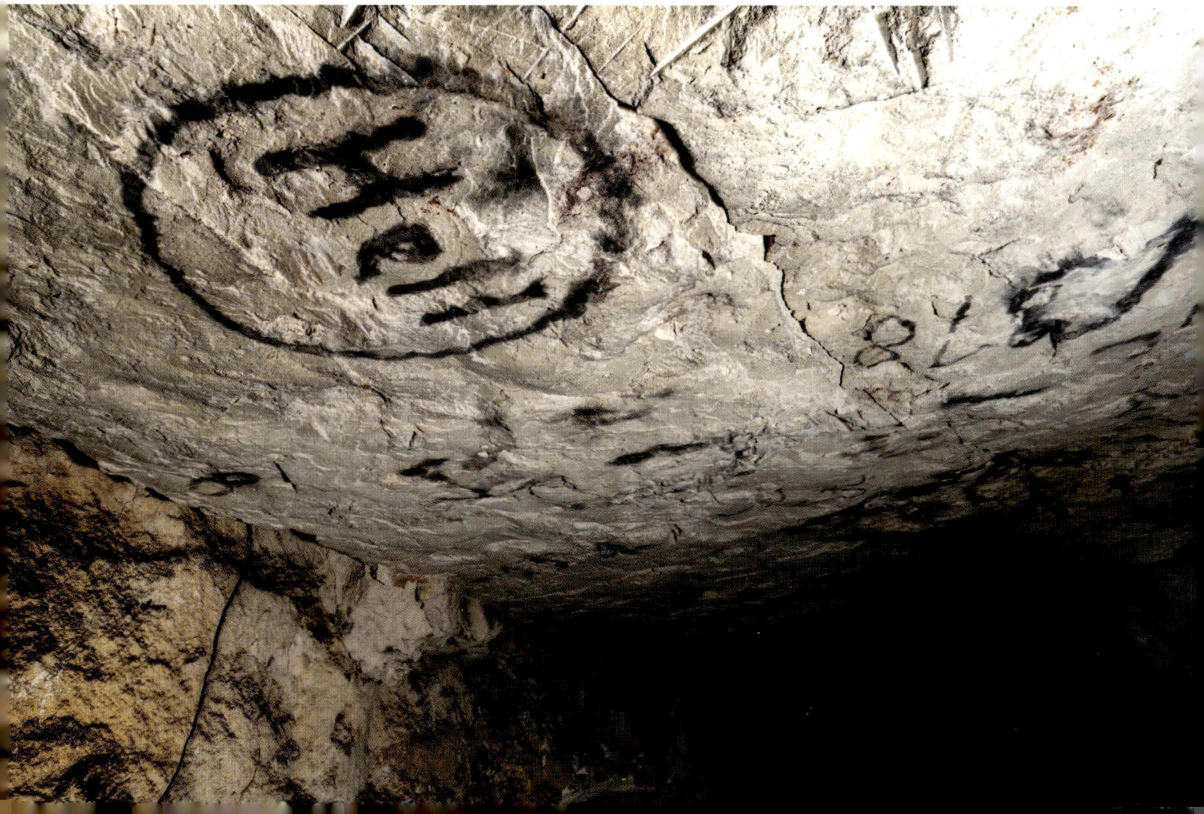

Overground Graffiti

First World War inscriptions aren't confined to underground sites. Soldiers left tens of thousands of traces on the walls of churches, farms and villages where they were billeted. Many have survived although scores disappear each year through renovation or erosion.

Carving was as easy here as in the souterraines because many of the buildings were constructed from the limestone extracted from local quarries.

Dominique Faivre, who has been researching wartime graffiti in the Artois region around Arras since 1999, has identified more than 700 Canadian soldiers who left their names on village walls between December 1916 and May 1918

Around 75 per cent of the graffiti he has found is Canadian, 20 per cent British and the remainder French and other nationalities.

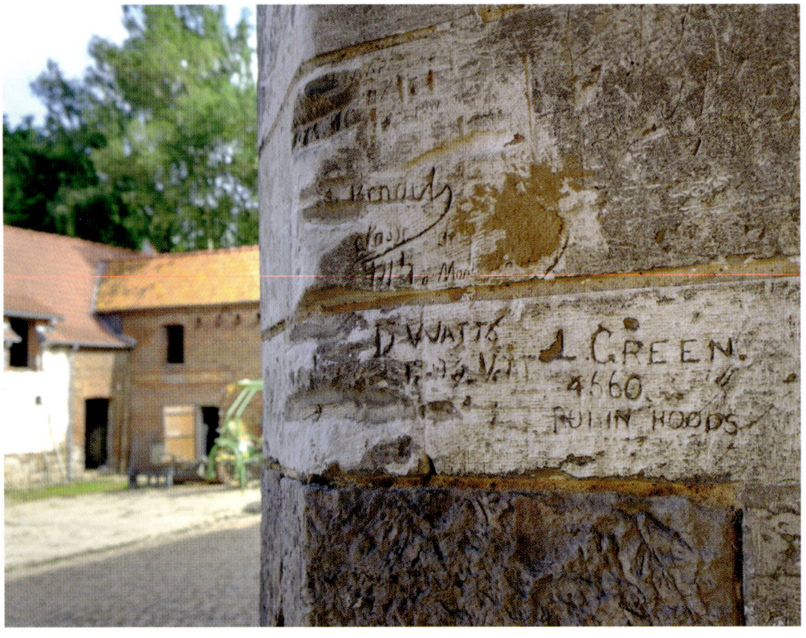

British soldiers' inscriptions on the wall of a farm in the village of Mont-Saint-Éloi, near Arras.

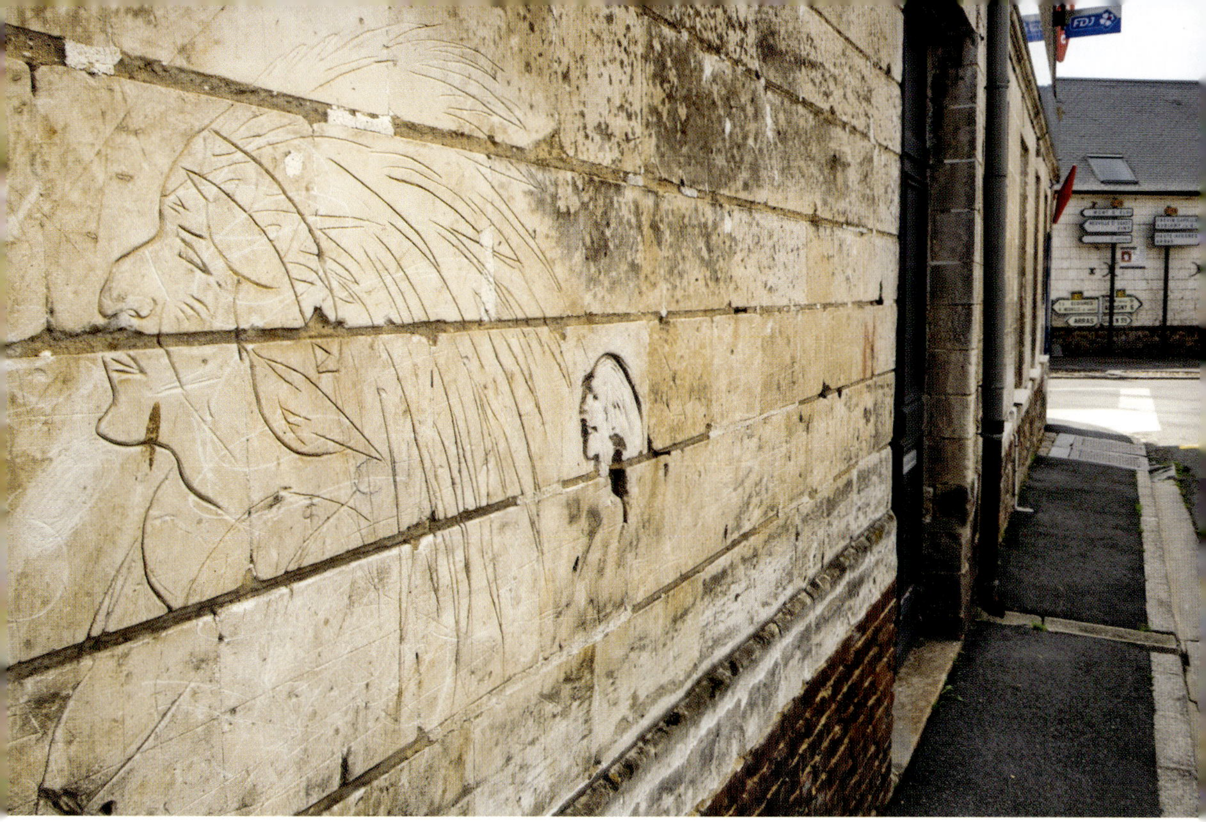

Carvings of Native Americans in the village of Acq.

Stroll through picturesque Artois hamlets like Bethonsart, Acq and Mont-Saint-Éloi and names of soldiers can still be seen on facades, along with regimental insignia and Native American profiles with grand headdresses.

In Bethonsart, one farm has a wealth of graffiti including a carving of a running Devil carrying a trident – the regimental badge of the Royal Winnipeg Rifles, nicknamed the Little Black Devils.

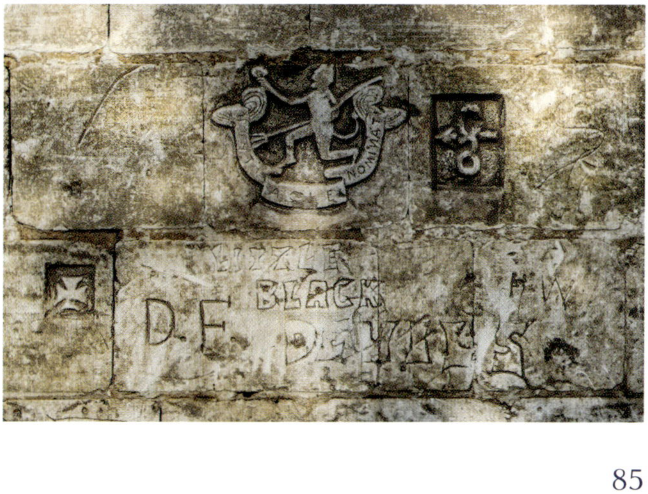

The regimental badge of the Royal Winnipeg Rifles, nicknamed the Little Black Devils, on the wall of a farm in Bethonsart.

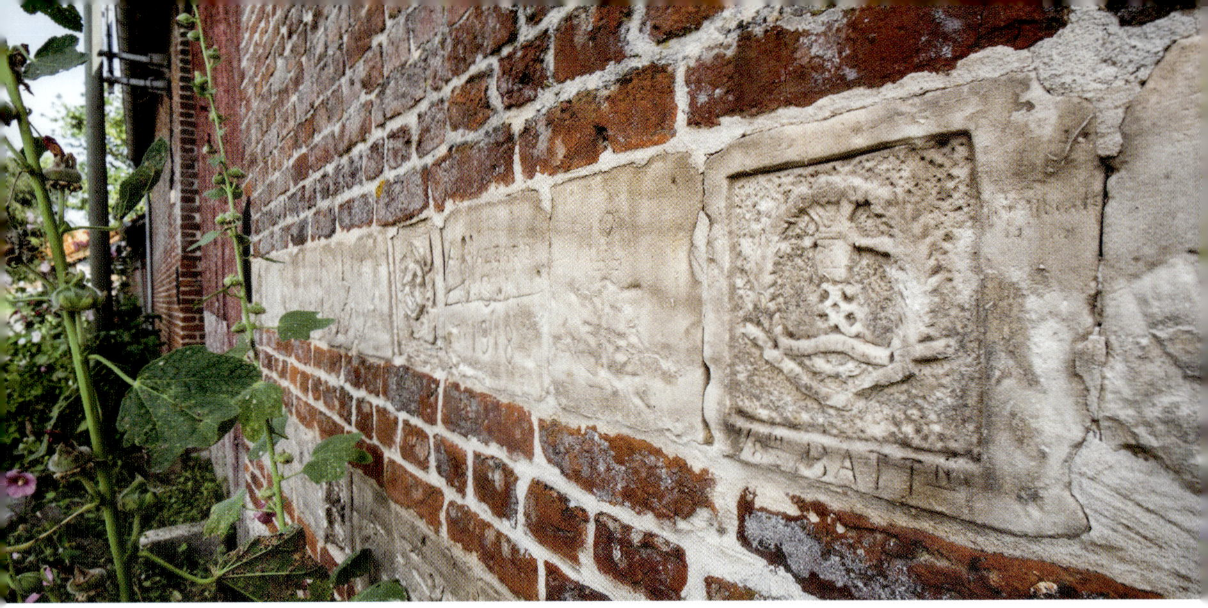

Regimental insignia preserved on a wall in Bethonsart.

A little more faded but still visible are the badges of the Duke of Cornwall's Light Infantry, the Leeds Pals (15th Battalion of the West Yorkshire Regiment) and the Royal Naval Nelson Battalion, among others.

The back of the sixteenth-century St Martin's Church in the hamlet of Ecoivres is covered with graffiti of all ages but the inscriptions left by soldiers from the First World War are carved deeper, with more commitment and the clear desire to leave a lasting trace in the stone.

They include William David Boag, a student from Ontario who enlisted at eighteen and inscribed his name and regimental number in fine writing on the church wall on 3 July 1918. He was killed just over a month later in an attack by the 4th Canadian Infantry Battalion at Beaufort-en-Santerre on the Somme. 'Casualties very heavy,' the battalion's war diary notes for that day. 'Many gallant acts were performed by all ranks in face of extremely severe machine gun fire.' William's mother, Alice Jane Boag of Barrie, Ontario, requested that the personal inscription 'The Lord is my shepherd, I shall not want,' be inscribed on his headstone in Bouchoir New British Cemetery.

Avril Williams, who runs the Ocean Villas tea rooms and guest house frequented by visitors to the Somme battlefields, has soldiers' inscriptions in her cellar, the only one still intact from the war in the village of Auchonvillers. It was an aid post for stretcher cases during the Battle of the Somme and she believes that one of the carvings, a badge engraved with a J and a C, was created by comrades of Private James Crozier of the Royal Irish Rifles, who went absent without leave from mud-swamped, rat-infested trenches near Serre on the last day of January 1916.

He was picked up a week later wandering aimlessly 40 kilometres from the headquarters of his division without his cap badge, pay book or rifle. Charged with desertion, he told his court martial that he could not remember what he did but that he had been in a daze and suffered from pains throughout his body. A doctor who examined him after the court martial pronounced him fit.

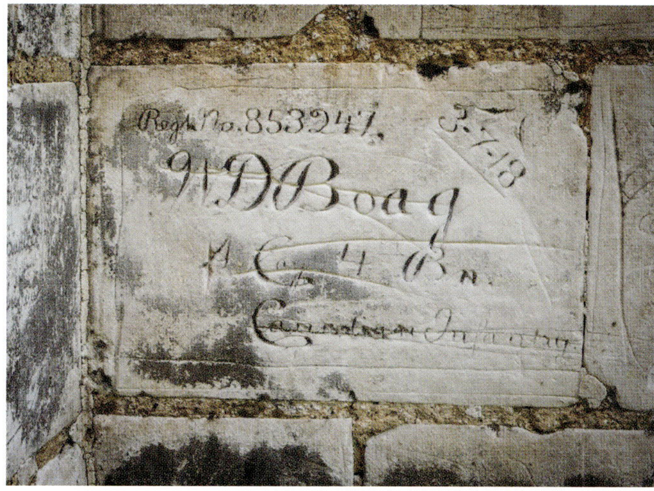

William David Boag was killed a month after carving his name into the outer wall of St Martin's Church in Ecoivres.

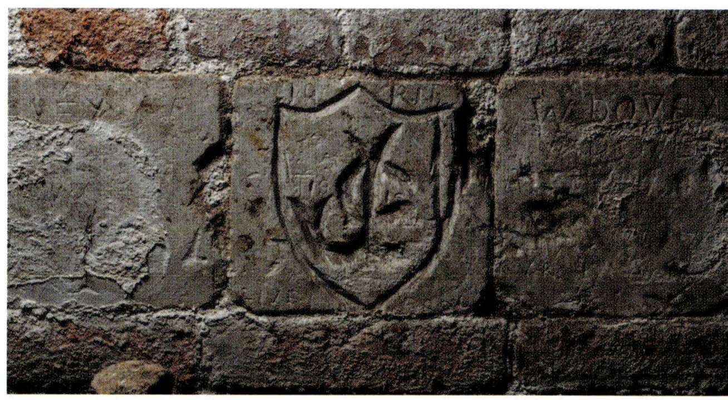

The carving that may be in honour of Private James Crozier, on Avril Williams' cellar wall in the Somme village of Auchonvillers.

Crozier, an apprentice at the Harland & Wolff shipyard, had enlisted in September 1914, weeks after the outbreak of war, with dreams of adventure, escaping poverty and becoming a hero. His mother Elizabeth had tried to stop him but an officer, Frank Percy Crozier, no relation, had assured her that he would look after her son and 'see that no harm comes to him.' He broke that promise. As James' commanding officer, Lieutenant Colonel Crozier was asked to give his recommendations at the court-martial and sealed his fate by writing that he believed 'the crime was deliberately committed with the intention of avoiding duty' shortly after another soldier who had gone absent had had his sentence reduced to hard labour. James Crozier was sentenced to execution by firing squad.

Plied with alcohol the night before his execution, he was unable to stand when he was taken out at dawn on 27 February. He was hooked on to the post 'like dead meat in a butcher's shop,' wrote Crozier, who eventually became a brigadier general before turning into a pacifist.

The firing squad made up of soldiers from James Crozier's own regiment shot wide and an officer strode up to kill him with a single bullet. James Crozier was among 306 servicemen shot by the British Army for offences such as cowardice or desertion. It took until 2006 for the government to decide that they should be pardoned.

A Case for UNESCO

Many of the more than 10,000 inscriptions and carvings found in underground sites along the Western Front are destined to fade from the walls, be buried by tunnel collapses or remain unseen in the blackness of forgotten quarries.

At Bouzincourt, dampness is causing pencil inscriptions to dissolve into illegibility and a quarter are deemed to be in a poor or very poor state of conservation.

At Naours, the rub of a tourist's shoulder against the wall can wipe out a 100-year-old story.

Profile of a French soldier from the 64th Infantry Regiment (see collar) at Froidmont. The unit fought under Napoleon at Austerlitz and dates back to 1672.

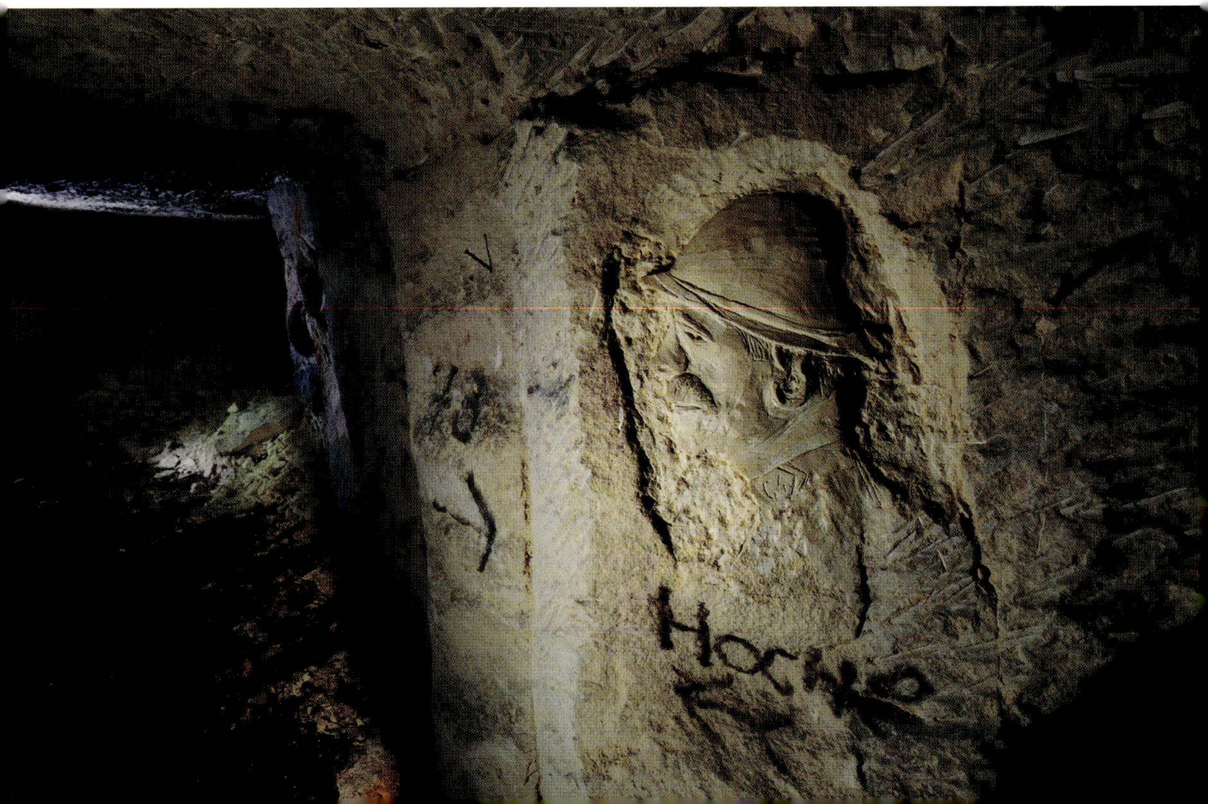

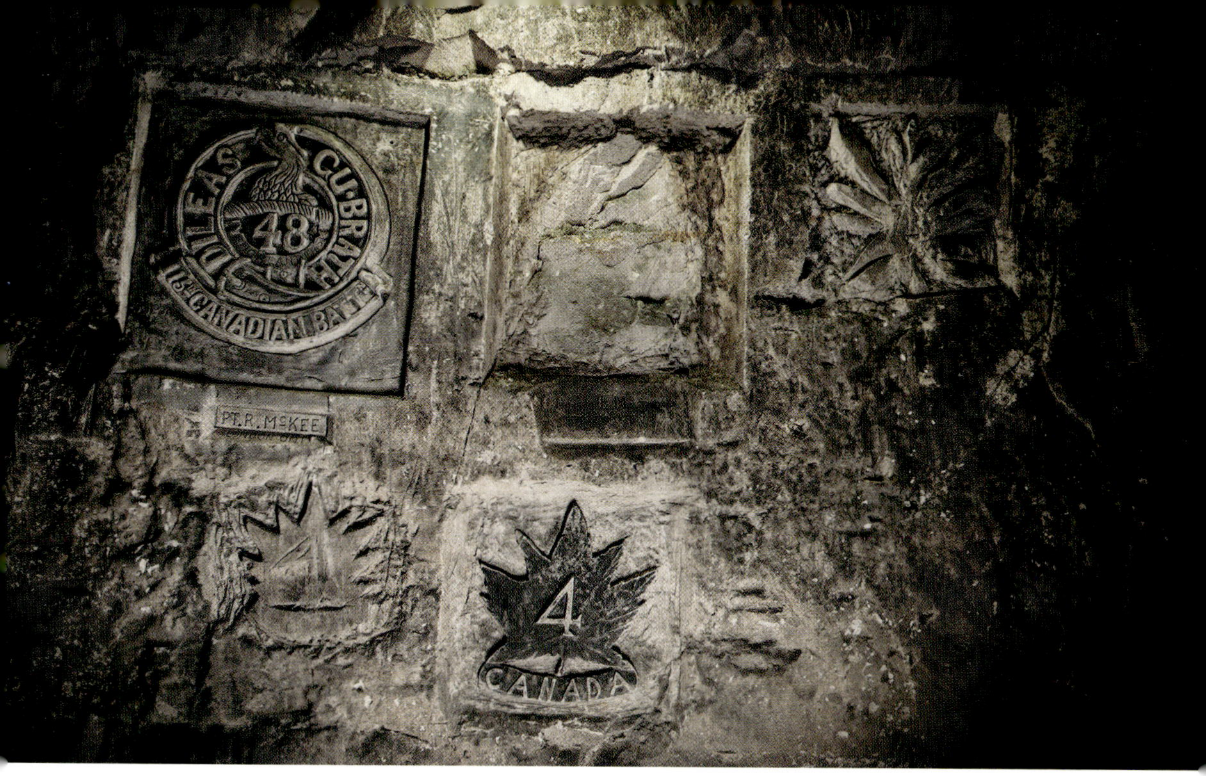

Above: A carving has evidently been cut out of this wall in the Maison Blanche quarry.

Right: The guide and local councillor Dr Arnaud Durier, lighting a candle in a groove cut by soldiers in Maison Blanche.

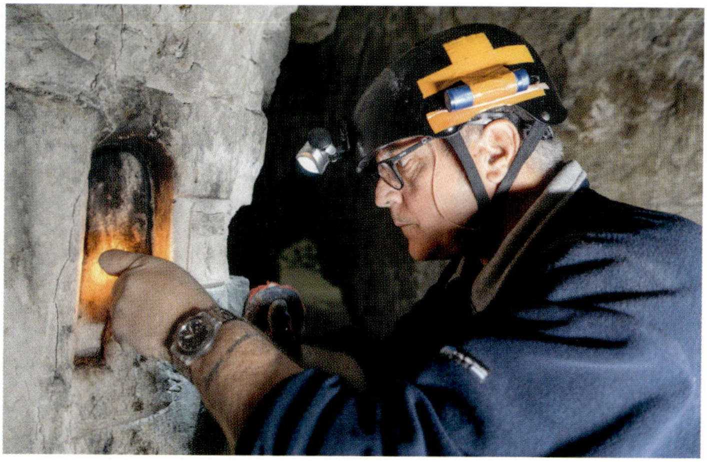

One of the most precious galleries of soldiers' art, the Maison Blanche quarry, is at risk from water ingress and tremors caused by heavy farm machinery passing overhead.

The souterraines are also vulnerable to looters in search of collectibles. Some are protected by committed volunteers who are kept busy replacing locks and repairing gates and grilles. Others are at the mercy of intruders. At the Rouge-Maison quarry near Vailly-sur-Aisne, some carvings have been defaced with modern spray can graffiti, revealing a disrespect that even the combatants, after years of trying to kill one another, didn't show for each other's inscriptions.

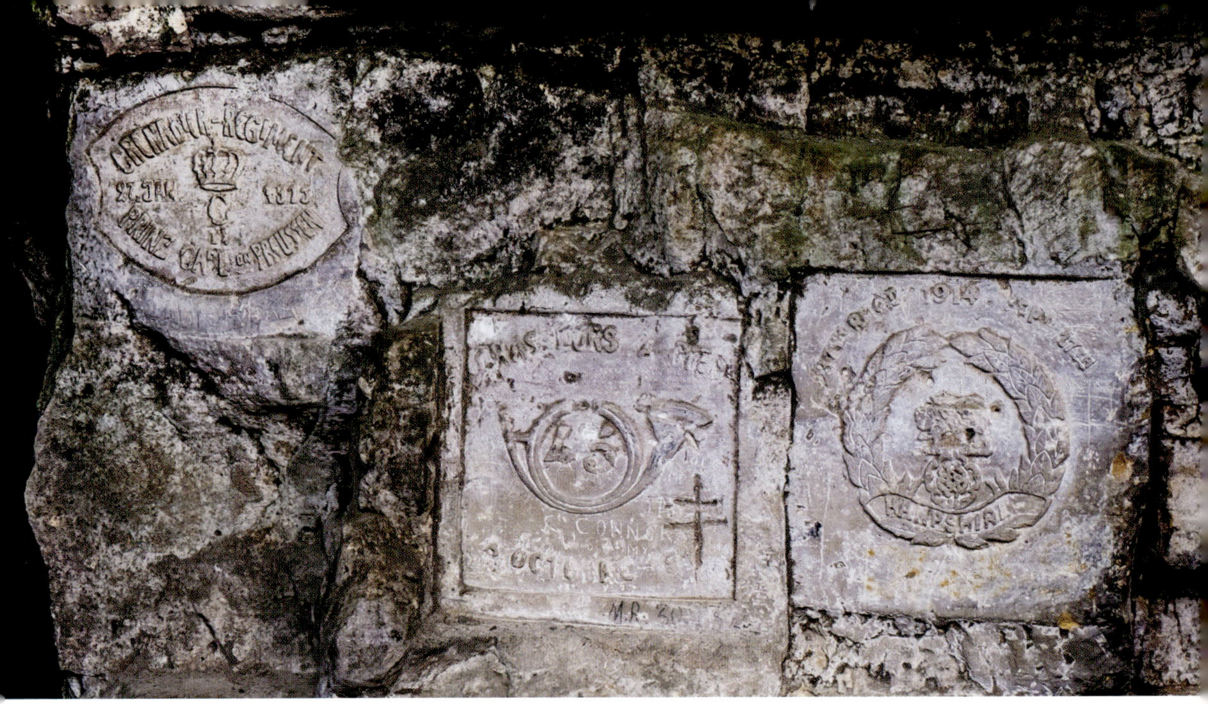

Regimental insignia carved by (from right to left) British, French and German units on a pillar of a quarry in the Aisne department. The badge of the Hampshire Regiment on the right was created by Sergeant Alfred Brisley in September and October 1914. A few days later the French 45h Battalion of the Chasseurs à Pied moved in. The Prinz Carl von Preussen Grenadier Regiment took over the quarry in January 1915. The German troops did not deface the carvings.

In recent years, archaeologists including Gilles Prilaux have recognised the urgency of recording the sites and their contents. Prilaux's discovery of the wealth of inscriptions at Naours in 2014 has triggered a wave of fresh research into Western Front graffiti which has included systematic cataloguing of inscriptions and creating 3D digital imagery of souterraines – that, say researchers, is probably the only way to keep the soldiers' testimony alive for posterity and ensure broad access to it.

Prilaux has obtained public funding for research projects involving students, both French and international, and devised a museum about the Naours graffiti that was opened in 2020 to tell the stories of the men who made their mark there.

Fellow archaeologist Vincent Faivre has recorded and analysed the over 1,000 inscriptions at Bouzincourt in a valuable contribution to research.

In some locations, the graffiti seems safe. At Montigny, which like the Naours underground village is open to the public, the local association 'La Machemontoise' proudly nurtures its trove of sculptures in a stunning setting of vast caverns and towering rock pillars so thick that they will surely stand the test of time. After all, stone has been quarried here since the Dark Ages.

At the Wellington Quarry under Arras, traces left by the soldiers can be seen from modern walkways in a subterranean museum opened in 2008 to display a section of the kilometres-long tunnel network adapted and dug in preparation for the 1917 Battle of Arras.

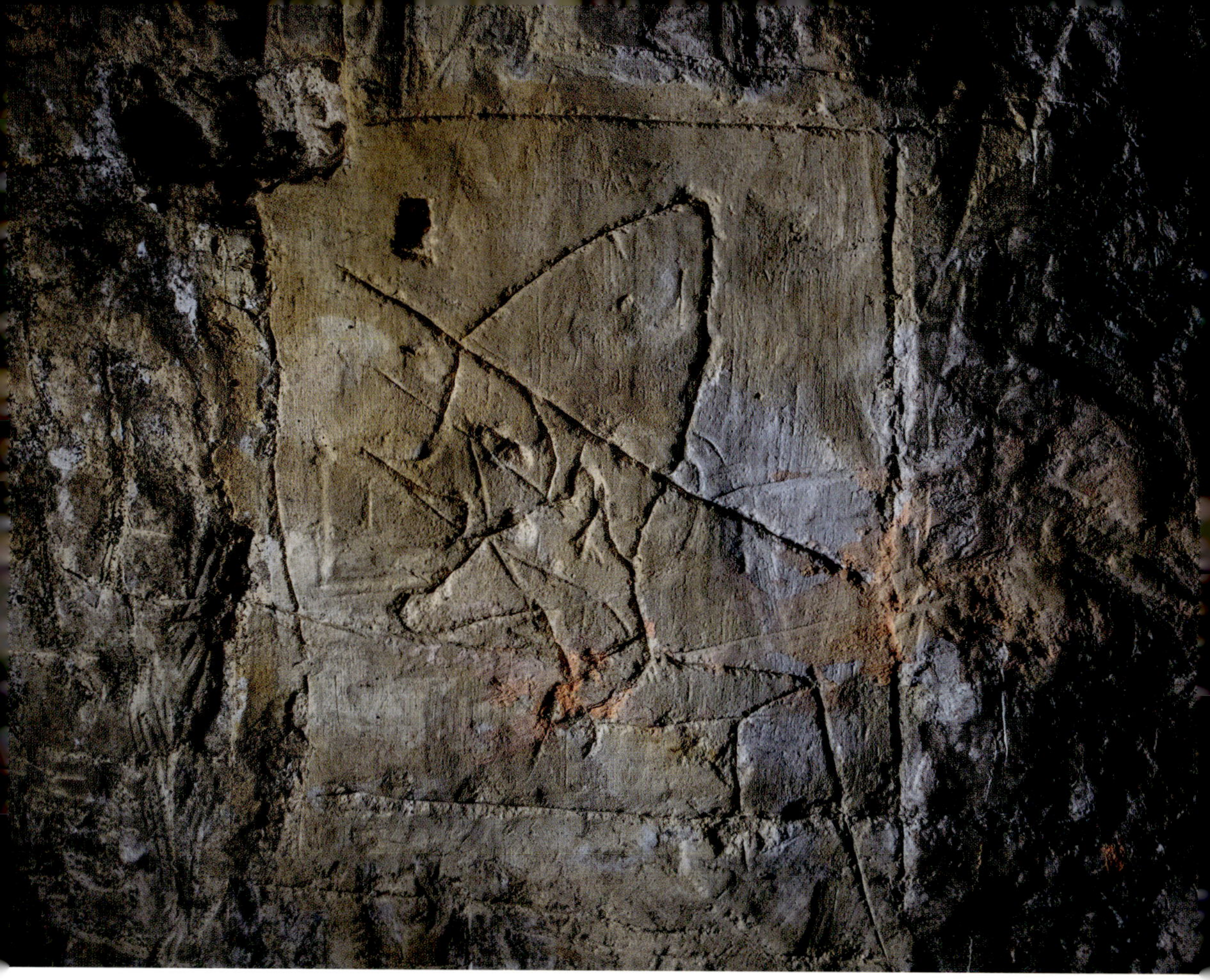

Above: A Canadian carving in the Wellington Quarry under Arras.

Right: The Wellington Quarry in Arras is a tourist attraction.

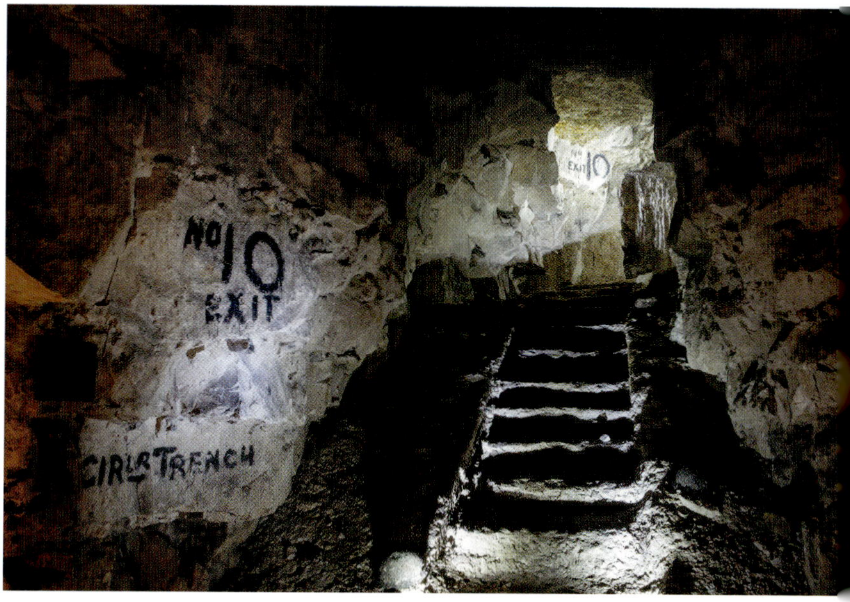

However, mass tourism is out of the question for the vast majority of souterraines given the difficulty and danger of entering them and the fragility of their carvings. Local heritage associations have been alerting public authorities and landowners to the significance of the sites since the 1980s. Their efforts led to a dozen quarries being listed as historic monuments in the 1990s. But there is no nationally funded or EU-funded programme to protect them.

There should be. These souterraines that became canvases for men from many nations in a cataclysmic conflict that shaped the troubled world we live in today must surely qualify for classification as a UNESCO World Heritage site.

Public remembrance of the First World War may have culminated with the 2014 to 2018 centenary events. But the graffiti now emerging offers a new perspective on the conflict.

Not only by shedding light on the fates of thousands of individuals. And not only by illustrating the strength of the human spirit in the face of horror. But by bringing us face to face with a young generation far less fortunate – and reminding us of the lessons of their sacrifice.

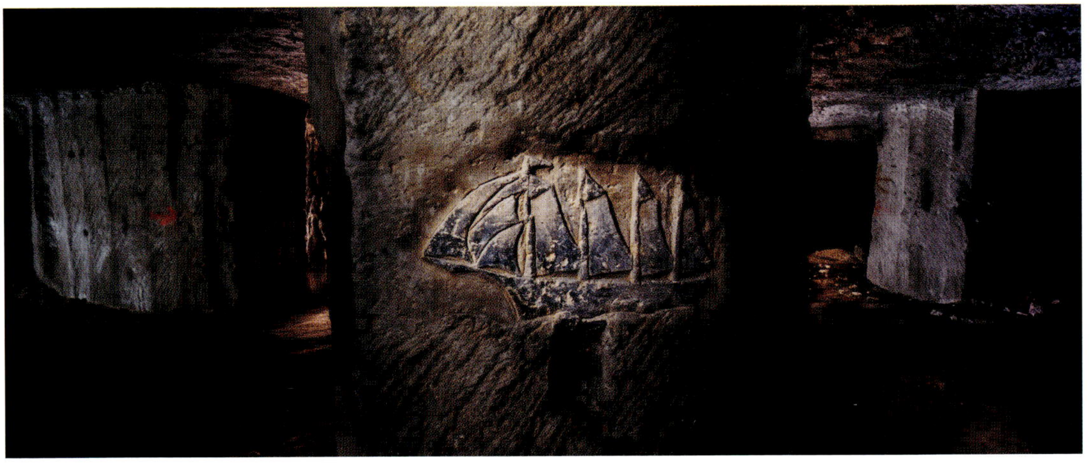

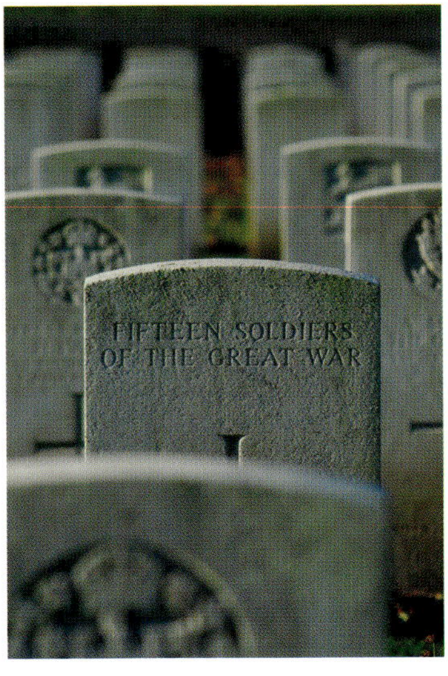

Above: A hopeful ship in a sea of darkness, carved by a soldier in a quarry near the Chemin des Dames.

Left: British war graves in Connaught Cemetery, the Somme.

Photographic Credits and Bibliography

Photographic credits

All photos taken by David Crossland except where stated.

Thank you to the French museum La Contemporaine, the Bordeaux Municipal Library and the Bundesarchiv German Federal Archive for their help in obtaining original photos.

Bibliography

Baldridge, C. LeRoy, *I Was There With The Yanks on the Western Front* (New York and London, G.P. Putnam's Sons, 1919)

Bratten, Jonathan, *To The Last Man A National Guard Regiment in the Great War, 1917–1919* (Fort Leavenworth, Combat Studies Institute Press, 2020)

Bridge, Kathryn, *Phyllis Munday, Mountaineer* (Lantzville, XYZ Publishing, 2003)

Coombs, Rose E. B., *Before Endeavours Fade* (Barnsley, After the Battle, 2010)

Crozier, Brigadier-General Frank Percy, *The Men I Killed* (London, Michael Joseph, 1937)

Dartnall, Herbert J.G., *Lost in the Mists Leslie Russell Blake, Mawson's Cartographer and Hero of Pozières* (Melbourne, Australian Scholarly Publishing, 2014)

Deneuville, Alain, *Bethonsart Un Petit Village d'Artois* (Bethonsart, 2018)

Edmonds, Adrian Henry, war diary. Usage permission kindly granted by the Estate of Adrian Henry Edmonds.

Faivre, Vincent, *Graffiti & Inscriptions de la Grande Guerre: l'Identité Souterraine des Combattants dans les Entrailles des Muches de Bouzincourt* (Amiens, Master's Thesis, History, Civilisations, Heritage History and Archaeology at the University of Amiens, 2018/2019 academic year)

Hardier, Thierry, *Traces rupestres de combattants (1914–1918)* (Senones, CRID 14-18/EDHISTO, 2021)

Lambot, Lucette et Bernard, *Marius Corpait Léopold Marechal Deux artistes pendant la Grande Guerre* (Machemont, Editions la Machemontoise, 2015)

Leonard, Matthew, *Beneath the Killing Fields* (Barnsley, Pen & Sword Archaeology, 2016)

Mayoux, Pierre, *Paul Doncoeur Aumônier militaire* (Arcueil, Les presses d'Ile de France, 1966)

McWilliams, J.L.; Steel, R. James, *The Suicide Battalion* (Leeds, Sapere Books, 2020)

Middlebrook, Martin, *The First Day on the Somme* (London, Penguin Books, 1984)

Moan, Ralph T., war diary, *My Trip 'Over There'*

Pamart, Jean-Luc, *Le Paysan des Poilus* (Sainte-Marguerite-sur-Mer, Éditions des Équateurs, 2004)

Prilaux, Gilles (Text) and Bossut, Dominique (Photographs), *Graffiti & bas-reliefs de la Grande Guerre* (Paris, Michalon/Inrap, 2018)

Prilaux, Gilles; Beuvin, Mathieu; Fiechtner, Michael ; Fiechtner. Donna, *The Silent Soldiers of Naours* (London, New Holland Publishers, INRAP, 2017)

Richards, Frank, *Old Soldiers Never Die* (Uckfield, The Naval & Military Press, 2009)

Rubin, Richard, *Back Over There* (New York, St. Martin's Press, 2017)

Sibley, Frank Palmer, *With the Yankee Division in France* (Boston, Little. Brown, and Company, 1919)

Vatel, Hervé; Boittiaux, Michel, *Le Graffiti des tranchées* (Vic-sur-Aisne, Soissonnais 14-18, 2008)

Walker, Stephen, *Forgotten Soldiers: The Story of the Irishmen Executed by the British Army during the First World War* (Dublin, Gill & Macmillan, 2007)

Weber, Thomas, *Islands of Peace* (working title), to be published

Archives and Websites

Ancestry.co.uk
Australian War Memorial
Canadian Great War Project
Commonwealth War Graves Commission
Findmypast.com
French Culture Ministry database Grand Mémorial
French Defence Ministry database Mémoire des Hommes
Forces War Records
German Bundesarchiv Federal Archives
German First World War digitised 'Verlustlisten' casualty lists
Library and Archives Canada
Prisoners of the First World War ICRC Historical Archives
Soissonnais 14-18
State Library of New South Wales
State Library of Queensland
The National Archives (UK)
Virtual War Memorial Australia
Volksbund German War Graves Commission

Acknowledgements

I am deeply grateful to the archaeologist Gilles Prilaux, project manager at the research organisation EPCC Somme Patrimoine, Vincent Faivre, head of archaeological operations for the Calais region, and Vincent's father Dominique Faivre, an expert on wartime graffiti.

I would also like to thank Gilles Chauwin, the president of the Association du Chemin des Dames, and David Hedges, a member of the Durand Group.

Thank you also to Arnaud Durier, Martyn L. Gorman of the University of Aberdeen Zoology Museum, the French historian Thierry Hardier and Avril Williams, the owner of the Ocean Villas tea room and guest house in Auchonvillers. Jean-Luc Pamart and Hervé Vatel showed me the quarries of Confrécourt. Benedikt Geuchen, his brother Paul and Michel Duflos guided me around the Montigny labyrinth.

Caroline Lebourgeois, the director of the Naours underground city, could not have been more helpful. Battlefield guide Isabelle Blake showed me rarely seen inscriptions at Naours.

I am grateful to the historian Marie-Christine Allart in Neuville-Saint-Vaast and to Arnaud Battefort and Bernard Cagniet in Vailly-sur-Aisne.

Sandra Montgomery, the great-niece of Victoria Cross winner Samuel Meekosha, provided valuable information and photos, as did Ross Fuller, the nephew of Corporal Alister Ross, and Mike Ambler, the grandson of Aleck Ambler. The author Adrian Hellwig shared information about his late friend Harold Raymond George Edwards, who guarded the Red Baron's body. Thank you also to Emma Clayton, a journalist at the *Bradford Telegraph & Argus*.

Frederick Willmann, vice-president of the research association ARRRAS, showed me a fascinating quarry in Habarcq. I am also grateful to the artist Karen Begg of the Studio West Bronze Foundry & Gallery in Canada.

Thank you to Captain Jonathan Bratten, Command Historian for the Maine National Guard, and Alain Deneuville who showed me inscriptions left by Allied soldiers in Bethonsart.

Diane Tempel-Bornett and Ilka Borowski of the Volksbund, Germany's war graves commission, helped me research the fate of German combatants.

I would also like to mention my friend Tony Roddam, a keen photographer, pilot and fellow Francophile with whom I have visited the Western Front many times.

My wife Madeline, a journalist, was a critical sounding board. My mother, Kathleen Crossland, kindled my interest in the First World War long ago by telling me about the adventures of her father, Charles Stone, who emigrated to Canada and became a lumberjack. He joined the 13th Battalion of the Canadian infantry, the same unit as Aleck Ambler. I scoured the area for a trace of my grandfather. I haven't found one. But I will keep looking.

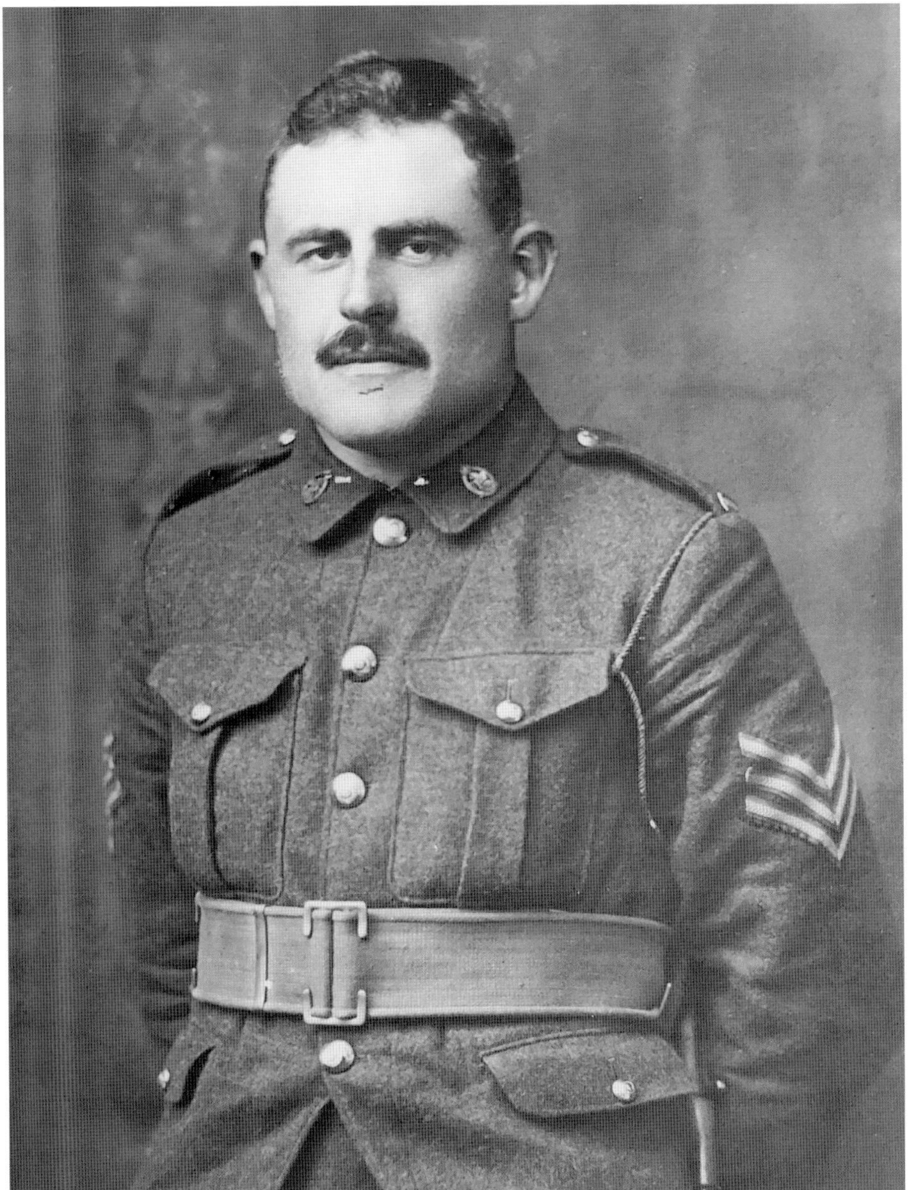

My grandfather Charles Stone. (Photo provided courtesy of Kathleen Crossland)